Introduction

I don't come from much. Born near know where, modest circumstances and told not to expect better. That was a long time ago and far away. I write this from a tropical island by my swimming pool, surrounded by opulence. Yesterday I was told my return flight was cancelled to my other home. I have a special card with a special number and I made a call. I was granted the last business class seat out for sixty dollars. There are privileges to be had. Power to influence. To go where you wish and when.

So, you are interested in becoming part of the 1%? Are you sure? All that money what would it offer you? How big can you dream? You could buy whatever you wanted. You would not have to work. You could go on vacation and never come back. People might be nicer to you. Some would be jealous of you. That might be a nice change. You could go all id and act as spoiled and rotten as you want and believe that you face no consequences.

You could help others in meaningful ways. Help them with their education, buy them a home, start a business. You could fund charities that are finding cures for world threatening viruses, green energy and help children in need.

You could surround yourself with the best esthetic. Beautiful art, luxurious furniture and a beautiful home. A home that inspires you every day with its peaceful setting, magnificent views, and rooms to welcome and entertain friends and family. You could set yourself free from time consuming grunt work and give yourself meaningful experiences with the best teachers of art, literature and business. You could travel to see art, culture, history and geography.

Or you could lie around all day in a bathrobe eating bon bons watching television. Choose wisely or not. You get to dream bigger dreams and have the means to make it all come true for yourself and others. Or not.

What would your dream be of being the 1%? Take a moment, let yourself dream.

The 1% who are they?

But who are the 1%? Let's start with their assets, that is easiest. The 1% have more wealth than 99% of the population. Breath taking no brainer. You're welcome. But there are greater assets to the 1% then the money in the bank. There is a way of thinking, and different choices to be made and a different way of behaving. If a person made the transition to becoming the 1% there is something about them that is exceptional and more so than a net asset balance sheet. To make the transition there has to be a journey taken where you put yourself in situations that require more risk. There are characteristics developed in your personality and knowledge that you have that get you from the 99% to the 1%.

To take a deep dive into this 1% idea, let's look further than what they got in the bank. As the 1% you have more choices then almost everyone else. Choice is a profound luxury. You can choose to work or not and have more say about the terms of your work. Because you have enough money to support yourself you are less likely to tolerate an abusive work or home environment. People like to work weather they need to or not. But what people hate about work is an abusive environment. With economic freedom you do not have to put up with manipulation and bullying behavior. Being part of the 1% has a profound effect on the nature of your relationships with others. You do not have to conform to others. The constraints in your life are not imposed on your time, or activities. People cater to you, not the other way around. You get to make the rules for yourself and often for others. Whoever has the gold makes the rules. Golden Rule. Live this way for years and it is a profoundly different way to live. If you were raised in a 1% household it becomes how you see yourself in this world. You learn a different language, you have a different belief system, a different set of expectations, in general higher expectations and sense of entitlement. If you believe you deserve more you will make choices accordingly. You will expect treatment from others fitting with an entitled mind set. You will put yourself in situations where you expect more. I believe you do not have to be raised by 1% parents to learn what they know, to chose what they chose. Anyone can learn and anyone can change their behavior.

If you are uncomfortable with the idea of becoming "entitled" good you have a conscience. But the sense of entitlement can be good. Having expectations according to what you are capable of, what you have achieved is okay. A person who has huge expectations of others and brings nothing to the relationship, that sense of entitlement is very harmful to any relationship and is annoying and disgusting.

Being part of the 1% is not a guaranty of bliss. One fellow who was part of the 1%, an heir to a manufacturing empire, had problems in his relationships. He was used to having people around him who saw him as the boss. People often tried to anticipate what he wanted and went out of their way to please him. This is a very attractive way to exist in relationships with others when you are the boss. However, relationships with a spouse or friends usually break down when they are that one sided. A spouse with any individuality and intelligence will not accept this one-sided relationship and if they do, they are just there for the money. Some 1%-ers enjoy a one-sided relationship so much it makes them try to impose this style of relationship with others with inevitable disaster. Ask any divorce lawyer. In the media it is often reported the drama of the 1%'s relationships because the imbalance of power in their relationships leads to chaos. Their relationships have a higher chance of narcissism that can more easily lead to relationship break down.

The 1% have subtle ways of segregating themselves from the 99%. They sound like they are speaking the same language, but if you listen carefully, they are speaking a language within our language. They say things that tip off others that they are also part of the 1%. For example, in every city there is a neighborhood for the 1%. People from these neighborhoods do not say to strangers that they are from these wealthy areas they hang-back, they don't disclose this information. There is a way of phrasing where they live, it is like a code. In one city the 1% live in a neighborhood called Rosedale. This is a neighborhood of mansions and beautiful parks that the rich have lived in for one hundred years. People that have lived in this beautiful, tree lined street area do not say they live in Rosedale they choose to say where they live by giving the name of one of the streets that run through the neighborhood. One of these streets is called Mount Pleasant. People from Rosedale say they live in the "Mount Pleasant area." If you live in the neighborhood, you would know what this phrase means. It means you live in Rosedale and you know the cultivated language of the neighborhood. You have got the secret handshake. One woman from this area was asked what kind of car her husband drives, she replied that he drove a sports car. This is code for Porsche. When asked about what kind of work one man has, he replied that he had a desk job. He was CEO of a major corporation of which he was a principal owner. Get it, it is the language of the 1%. People learn languages. But access to the 1% is guarded and their way of thinking is not easily accessible unless you know where to look.

The 1% have a concern that others may want to know them with arterial motives. People of the middle class will brag about meeting a person of the 1%, explaining how they met So and So 1% person who is wealthy and known for Such and Such. How annoying and embarrassing. Also, people can be jealous and mean about what others have when they have not. People of the 1% can be used to influence or taken advantaged of financially. For example, marriage partners for the 1% are more scrutinized when they fall outside of the 1% due to fear of having met a "gold digger." This is why the prenup was invented. Half of the 1% assets could be a prize ticket to the 99%.

The 1% have symbols of what they are. To the middle and lower class these symbols appear to be coveted items that are only available to the 1% through exclusive stores in exclusive city areas Rodeo Drive, Madison Ave, Seville Row, Champs Aliases. This is true but expensive items are more than they appear to the lower class. These items tell a story, they are a metaphor that separates the 1% from the rest. The items signify a divide between us and them, the haves and the have nots. These items signal a knowledge base an understanding of what it takes to be the 1% and maintain that place in our society. Rich people's stuff are designed to impress, awe others. These items are rare, and exclusive to the wealthy and therefore convey a sense that the owners are special and important. The objects of wealth are to convey who is more powerful.

At Versailles in France there is a room 100 feet long called the Hall of Mirrors. The king of France, Louis the Fourteenth would sit on his elevated throne at the end of the Hall of Mirrors. When the king wanted to show the power he had, when he wanted to humble a visitor, he would have the visitor walk the one hundred feet of this grand room to show his visitor who was the supreme ruler. Who gets to be the boss, make the choices, who gets to decide? What is more important, to have a room such as the Hall of Mirrors or to have the power of the person who owns the Hall of Mirrors? Having a shiny bobble is nice. Who holds the power in the relationship is more valuable. Being well off to the 99% means you get to go shopping for what you want. To the 1% having wealth means you get to decide, more than others, for yourself and others. Being part of the 1% is about having power.

Winning a large lottery only makes you part of the 1% financially. Having a lot of money does not mean you will keep it or understand what it took to get it or the great possibilities having great wealth can give you. If you have not earned your wealth, you can easily lose it because you have not learned the skills to acquire it and keep it. If you did not grow up in a 1% family you probably have not heard the language of the 1% and have not learned the nuance of this way of speaking and thinking. People that win a lottery and move into a 1% neighborhood are often not accepted. They don't speak the language, they do not know the culture. Years ago, there was a TV show called the Beverly Hillbillies about a Tennessee Hillbilly family that struck oil obtained 25 million dollars and moved to Beverly Hills, a 1% neighborhood. They got into hilarious trouble because they did not know the 1% ways. On a weekly bases they had countless misunderstandings as to how to live their lives compared to the 1%. Even people that grow up in a 1% household do not always gain the knowledge or the skills it takes to stay inside the 1%. Often the second and third generation after the family became the 1% lose the money and they do not know how to find their way back to the 1% way of life.

Having a middle class is crucial to our democratic capitalist way of life. The middle class is the back bone, the structure that holds our way of life together. The 1% needs the values and self-discipline of the 99%. We cannot all be the 1%, who is going to ask if you want fries with that burger. The middle class have learned to work within a company, to show up on time, to follow direction, to not challenge authority or rules to not have an original thought outside of the corporate, social way of thinking. The middle class's language includes phrases such as "if that was such a good idea someone would have thought of that before you." Translation, you will not have an original idea. Do not take risks, stay inside the ideas given to you. In an ant colony you have simple tasks that keep the colony working. Do your task, do not invent new tasks, do what is expected of you. Civil Servants are the example of the middle-class person. They follow procedure, work for years within a system. They endure years of limited risk, following prescribed procedure. Their ability to endure sameness, and boredom is monumental. You can get so bored by the end of a civil servant career, as you wait for your modest pension, that you can seem depressed.

Inside the middle class you are taught "don't get too big for your britches." You are told that being well off is a sin. "It is easier for a rich man to get through the eye of a needle then into the kingdom of heaven." Being part of the 1% means you can be more generous to others than the average middle class person. One of the great joys for people either rich or poor is to give to others. In fact, giving to others can come back to reward you financially as well as emotionally. It is not uncommon for the 1% to have learned to give to others in a way that is more beneficial. Middle class donation money goes to feed people. 1% donations go to build infrastructure, construct roads, supply drinking water, and develop education. All of this goes toward changing a culture and create opportunity.

The middle class avoids risk. New ideas are bad ideas to be met with fear and suspicion. 1% thinking has an awareness that new ideas hold great potential and if you get in at the ground floor you will be exceptionally wealthy. Do you wish you would have bought Apple stock when it was first put on the stock market? The 1% are taught to take risks and manage their anxiety and the principals of risk management, in other words have a plan B. Middle class thinking just says take no risk but they miss opportunity.

Part of the limited way of thinking for the 99% is that work happens at a set time in a set place. So many constraining rules! The 1% are always working. At the country club, at the ski resort, the charity ball, the golf course, business happens. Your social life is mixed with your business life. When the Opera House of Paris was built it was designed as a place where the 1% would mingle, before and after the performance. The 1% could show off their finery, symbols of their wealth and power. This magnificent staircase in the lobby was designed as a grand open space so it could be a place to see and be seen. People met and made connections, business connections. The work of the 1% involves bringing ideas together with the people, money, and resources to make the ideas happen. You need the company of the other, with ideas, means, resources to make this happen. You accomplish this type of work formally in an office or informally in social situations. Middle class people work at a specific task that fits into the tasks that others are performing to have the wheel turn. They are a cog in a wheel that is moving. The 1% developed the idea of the wheel. They took the risk that the wheel is a good idea. The 1% decided the purpose of the wheel and put it in place and therefore they own the wheel and receive the larger profits for its output. The 1% own the patent for the wheel and they will license it to others. Do you understand the power of owning the wheel?

In England the 1%, also known as the aristocracy, owns a great deal of land. They have owned land for hundreds of years and they have owned the most valuable land in the country. They have ninety-nine-year leases on this land. The leases get passed from generation to generation. The people who own the land are wealthy but they know their children and grandchildren will be wealthy too. Often the 1% are recession and depression proof they invest in resources that are immune to economic fluctuations. Their assets gain in value and they gain in income. The 99% just have income and have limited assets or limited assets that produce an income. The 99% need to work for as long as they can and might get a modest asset otherwise called a pension plan that will earn a modest income that will support them when they can no longer work. Many in the 99% do not have a pension and governments are aware of this and have government pensions to mildly sustain the 99% when they no longer can provide for themselves. Many middle-class people slip into poverty in their old age because they did not plan for their old age with enough of an invested asset to sustain themselves. What magical thinking did they have that led them to think they will somehow, in the most vulnerable time in their life, think they will survive economically.

The 99% have many ways to contain risk, to protect themselves. They have unions to bargain for their wages and benefits, they have defined pension plans and insurance policies that cover liabilities. The 1% have different safeguards economically and they can operate outside safety gates, because this is where great opportunities exist and they can more easily take risk because they have so much wealth. Their safety gate is having a big pile of assets and income that cannot easily disappear. They have access to the blue chip, or more secure investments that have more resilience to economic down turns. They can afford a variety of investments (called diversification) that limit their risk encase one investment goes bad. The 99% live with such passive safeguards outside of themselves and over time they make choices to stay where they are, safe with limited risk, not thinking outside the box of institutionalized safety. New ideas are not usually insurable. Unions promote sameness for all, equal pay for equal work but workers have different abilities and work ethics. The sound of union speak goes against the grain of the 1% way of thinking. Collective bargaining, equal pay and equal rights, and strikes are against the sensibility of the 1%. In the country of Cuba, equal pay and equal rights has played out in an extreme way for sixty years. Workers make about the same wage whether you are a doctor or a street cleaner. The level of education or responsibility in the job is not accounted for. The result is that highly educated people in Cuba often do not stay in their trained professions and change their work to the tourist industry where tips will give them more income than their trained profession. The possibility of a 1% group in the Cuban culture has been eliminated through government policy. However, extraordinary problems have occurred as a result. The economy of Cuba is very poor. Although the island of Cuba has much agriculture land it imports 70% of its food and many people in Cuba have trouble finding enough to eat.

What am I telling you to do?

So, what am I selling? What am I trying to get you to do? I am encouraging you to develop an economy outside your day job, outside the middle-class income and work. I am telling you to break out of being part of the 99%. Develop an income and asset building investment or business that will get you to be part of the 1%. Do this more for how this will develop you as a person and do it for the economic freedom. Develop something that is more than another job it is a quest. I am telling you to create an idea, one that you are responsible for that will substantially increase your personal wealth. Take your best creative ideas, your best work ethic, take a risk and make something, a business or an investment that gives you the most opportunity economically and for your personal development. Get the economic freedom and get a chance to increase your abilities as a person. Bam! Get it done. You have until Thursday.

Why do this?

You have a day job and you are tired when you come home from work and you need your weekends off. So why develop another source of income. What are you greedy? How much does a person need? You can only wear one shirt at a time. And this is risky. We are talking about risky investments that may or may not go anywhere. So why bother?

Earnest Hemingway wrote a book called the "Old Man and the Sea" is about a fisher man with very little means who goes out to sea and catches the greatest fish of his life but by the time he returns to shore the fish has been hunted by sharks and there is nothing left to show for his efforts. That's depressing. Why bother? He should have stayed at home. But think about it... What does the fisherman have but the great experience he gained in finding such a great fish? He has the knowledge of what it took to get that fish and he knows what strength he found in himself to fend off the sharks that took the great fish from him. He knows more about himself and life. He has had a great adventure and his life has more substance and meaning because he had this monumental experience. He is a bigger man. A better man.

Most parents want to give their children the tools to create a life for themselves to go beyond the safety of what they offer them. Parents help their children find in themselves their abilities to make their own life. Yes, you as the parent know more about the tragedies in life, the problems, and heartaches, but your job is to give them the tools to weather the storms. You provide them a good education so they can get a good job, earn a good living to provide for themselves the comforts of life. Teach them to look after themselves, eat properly, exercise so they are strong and healthy. Have them make good choices in relationships so they attract friends and family who love them and are kind to them. Some parents will teach their children to be economically independent and will provide them with financial means that allow their child to have the best opportunities this culture allows.

But some parents want to have extraordinary safety for their children. They block them from most experiences of risk so their children never learn to endure difficulties and find themselves ill prepared for the storms of life. Some children fail to launch. They never leave a parent's home, never find long term work or relationships. They stay inside the safety of the house they grew up in. A sad small life.

How much will you fail to launch in your life? How much will you stay inside of a protective bubble? For some with their abundance of intelligence, extravert personality, outstanding good looks, and strong work ethic, life's abundance will easily present itself like low hanging fruit. And then there is the rest of us who will have to get a second job to afford the ladder to get said fruit. For many it won't come easy. But that is good. You can develop what it takes to get what you dream of in your life.

It is like being a member of a special club when you meet the people who took the harder road in life, dug deeper into what they are about, and took the risks. They put more meaning in their life and found out more about themselves and what they are made of. They got to know who they are and even pushed to become more. More knowledgeable, more resilient, more capable.

It is like love.

"What do you get when you kiss a guy, you get enough germs to catch pneumonia, and when you do, he never phones you. I'll never fall in love again."

Well, that's sad. Love and relationships are high risk, not for the faint of heart and some, once they taste the burn of love, never go again. Lonely life. How much love and maybe heart ache will you have in your life, but it is it better to have love and lost then to never have...

Seeing how far you will go to develop the biggest economy for yourself is like how much love will you seek and how much hurt will you avoid. How much love will you want to seek in your life. How many close relationships. If one partner does not work out, will you pick up the pieces, try again or disappear, wall yourself off, or learn from the past mistakes, and go again.

Old buildings have a patina that can exist with time and the elements of life. One of my favorite things to do is walk the streets of Paris with a friend who lives in beautiful Paris. He tells me stories of the people and the buildings of that great city. He shows me the bullet holes from when the Nazis occupied the city. He shows me the worn steps of the old chapels where thousands of people entered to find comfort and solitude through times of prosperity, pestilence, war and celebration. He shows me the progress of the city through its complicated history of great achievement and disaster. It is the patina of the buildings that are the record of the great adventure of life this city has to explain. But what will be the patina of you? The grey hair, the wrinkles the memories and stories that you will have because you lived the fullest life possible. Because you developed yourself, took risk and created.

I have taken risks that many others would not and it has brought me hardship and joy. One risk is having dug into several great cities and created a life in these places. This has given me exceptional experiences that a tourist could never know. Not knowing the language of these places or the culture was considered a risk by others but not me. But the risk of falling outside the safety of the tourist bubble has been risky and a great source of personal learning and adventure. By choosing some cities to do business in, own a property, and develop friendships I have broken through the safety of the tourist bubble. I am given access to the essence, the true way of life and experiences of these places because I put "skin in the game." The artificial, contrived tourist bubble is something I have left far behind.

I remember being taken to a place in a foreign country that no tourist would find. A place so far off the grid of our technology, the internet, telephone, banking system and modern transportation. The road ended and we had to abandon the car, my cell phone had no service, no Google Maps was available and we were not there yet. It was as though one hundred years of technology had disappeared and no one I was with spoke English. Where I was taken was beautiful beyond words. So green, the land, the trees, the river. Green everywhere you looked expect for the crystal clear blue sky. And yes, there were animal sacrifices. You don't know what you got till it's gone, but maybe its replacement is a source of wonder and awe. The risk of disappearing off our technological grid, the walk away from all that was familiar was a great adventure. What would it be like to step outside of your familiar and see new possibilities? You also know more about who you are by getting so outside yourself and where you come from that you have a chance to know the influence of your culture on you and you can make the better choices.

If you have run a marathon in your life, you know things about yourself that you cannot read about in a book or see in a movie. No one can run a marathon for you. It's you, from start to finish. People can cheer you on but it's you who trains, endures the pain, feels the glory when you cross the finish line. Do you have the self-discipline, the DNA, the drive, did you make the time to train? Did you learn to encourage yourself even when you wanted to quit. Very few people have the natural DNA to go out and run a marathon. You have to train. Some must train longer and it is harder for them. Same race but you bring what you have to the race for good or bad. Some people have a natural physicality gift to more easily run a marathon. But that does not mean they will be the fastest. The person that trains more and has a stronger determination can out-perform the person with the natural runner's physic. With learning the right training methods, putting in the time, adjusting your diet, you can influence your chances of the time and enjoyment of the marathon. But it comes down to you, to develop your best chances. If you get injured, will you work at the healing process and get back in the training or race. Will you do more than one marathon or do you only have one in you. Did you make the experience the best it could be for you? If you complete a marathon that experience can never be taken away from you. It is yours and when you know other marathoners you have a common bond, you know their pain and their glory of what each other has done. The running of a marathon is a defined experience it is a yes or no. Reaching beyond having a regular job, creating your own economy, creating your own business, is harder to define. But if you have built an investment, you know what it took to create it and you see it in others and they see it in you. Being part of the 1% you can put a number evaluation on it just like there is a regulated distance to a marathon, but it is more than that. What you had to do to accomplish either the marathon or your entrance to the 1% is far greater than a number. You had to enhance yourself. The process of becoming more than what you started with, is the glory.

The book Johnathan Livingston Seagull is about flying higher and faster than rest. The loneliness and the thunderous glory of this experience.

So, let's get started. If you are interested in becoming part of the 1% hang on its going to be an adventure and a bumpy ride.

What works to get you to be part of the 1%?

It is the people around you who should give you the economic opportunities that you deserve. They should realize your special talents and open the doors to access great economic possibilities. Others having been holding you back and bad luck.

Ha Ha just kidding.

What do you got to do? You have to make changes to how you think to create a 1% sensibility. You must create your best self. Mediocrity, "it's good enough," will not do. You need to take risk. Go outside your usual, because your usual has only got you where you are, the 99% comfort zone. Learn the psychological ability to handle your fears, your anxiety so you can endure risk. You must learn leadership skills so you can use the expertise of others. Any love you have for being an introvert needs to be challenged. You need to learn to be effective. You need to make stuff happen. That is profound. Beat down your personal demons that stand in your way. Know what your personal roadblocks are, your internal bureaucracy and overcome it. You want to stop spinning in circles going know where and instead build momentum, accelerate, bust through obstacles. Waiting for someone or something to change, or give you permission to achieve, is no longer a consideration. It's you. You need to take responsibility. Procrastination you got no time for. You need to nurture your best creative thoughts and your stick-to-id-ness. You need to be a cunning warrior. Nothing, Nothing, Nothing can get in your way. Find your passion, your best motivation and launch your beautiful self out of the 99% and into owning your own economy.

You can be a person that watches a movie about unlikely heroes that fight the good fight, overcomes the toughest foe. You can watch the athlete challenge the formidable odds of winning. You can read the book that depicts the story of the insurmountable obstacles to win in the end or...it can be you. You. You can put yourself in a situation that expands what you are. Taking yourself out of the 99% is not easy. The gravitational pull to stay in the safety net of the 99% is strong.

"I just want to go home at night from work and not think about anything." A higher level of responsibility is what you want. It is this level of responsibility that grows a more resourceful person. The journey to becoming part of the 1% is not easy. It is full of adventure, risk and contra verse. How brave are you? How brave do you want to be?

Capitalism you were born into it, or were you?

You are part of a capitalistic society/culture. But are you really taking full advantage of the opportunities that are offered you? Probably not. There are cultures within cultures. Languages within languages. Do you embrace all aspects of all parts of the culture you have access to? It is like shopping for groceries. Do you shop the entire store or do you limit yourself? "I can't go down that isle. Only smart, rich, important people shop for those foods. I don't belong there." If you shop the full store what will happen? Will you go to jail? Do you think, you live on this planet earth and have access to all it has to offer, ideas, products, riches, opportunities or do you live just on your street in your home, in your neighborhood, in your city, state, country? When you, grocery shop do you say, "I cannot buy that fruit or vegetable it came from too far away, touched by a foreign person, who speaks a different language." Or "oh look kiwi are on sale, they came from New Zealand. I will get some fruit from there today but maybe one day I will go there. See what is going on." How much do you limit your access to all aspects of this beautiful capitalistic culture that you are part of because of a mind-set that just keeps you in a place that you do not belong in. Opportunities without borders. You can get food from everywhere on this planet in most cities. There are no boundaries of time zones, political borders, languages, cultures. But opportunities have fewer boundaries then what most people's mind accept. What are the borders you have artificially put on yourself? Think about it. What don't you let yourself do? What are your personal roadblocks that stop you from going where you want to go?

Your tax system, banking system, access to the best goods and services are available to everyone, but only a small percentage of the population take part in it. The 1%. You have more opportunities than you know. The tax system allows and even promotes people to become well off. If you make a lot of money, you pay a significantly smaller proportion of your money in tax. The more you make and the faster you make it, the tinier your proportion of tax owed. And if you have significantly more money there are so many more ways to shield your income and assets from paying tax. Have you heard of the phrase "the rich get richer and the poor get poor?" It's true. You are part of this system, are you going to get in on it or not? Anybody can buy caviar, but do you? Are you curious about what holds you back? Well get curious.

The bank system offers great big loans to people who have great big assets and enormous incomes. With big, giant loans you can make gigantic investments that can give you extra big giant over whelming returns. You should get in on this deal. Highly recommended. Most people have more assets and income than they are aware of. Yes, you do. There are many examples of people who come from nothing and become part of the 1%. Not impossible.

There is great knowledge available about the process that people do to transition to a bigger economic way of life. People have biographies, blogs, podcasts to document their transition to becoming more, not just economically but the process and changes they make personally to give them full access to the best economic opportunities of this culture. But this knowledge does not seem to be acted on by most people. The comforts of the middle class, the predictability, the low risk is seductive to staying inactive.

Knowledge about the transition from a middle-class life to a full economic life of this culture is available. This transition is not about being super intelligent it is more about a body of knowledge and a journey, a philosophy, a way of thinking that can be learned. It means a change of behavior, exchanging one set of habits for another. It is do able if you want. It can seem magical, mysterious and unacceptable or not. But it is more dramatic to believe, that somethings are out of boundaries, secretive, forbidden, exclusive. The journey to change, to becoming more is a great ride and one that gives much more to you than more money in the bank. The money is just a by-product.

Let me explain to you a philosophy of going from existing to thriving economically in this lovely capitalistic culture of ours.

I worked in a hospital for twenty-five years with a group of professionals and we all made about the same amount of money and we were all hired within a few years of each other. Over the years I lived below my means and saved my money and I invested my extra income. Most of my coworkers spent all their income and went into debt to buy things that lost value, like cars and big screen TVs. I invested my money in real estate that was undervalued and I added value to the properties by renovating these houses in what were "up and coming neighborhoods." Not only did the houses improve in value because of my renovation work but the neighborhoods became sought after places to live and the price of the properties increased in value exponentially. Good for me. Not only did I invest my money but I took the risk of borrowing money to invest in properties that went up in value. What I saved from my work income was enough to make serious investments. Yes, it was risky. Yes, it was exciting. I rarely watched TV. Real life was more exciting than watching a chase scene in an action, adventure movie.

When I quite my day job a number of coworkers told me, I was crazy. They warned me that I did not have enough money to quit work, I would be bored, I did not know what I was doing. I had kept my investment life somewhat quiet at work, but now that I was quitting, I was not so concerned about my coworker's opinions. After weeks of enduring numerous warnings of the poor choice I was making I told the most adamant predictors of impending doom how much I was worth. They never talked to me again. Since I left work, I have made more money in the last few years then in the last twenty-five years at the day job. I should have quit sooner. I was not brave enough and more importantly I did not completely understand the thinking of the 1%.

Only after seeing the results of my choices over time and how these choices got me to a different place economically did I understand that I was onto something. I am rarely the smartest guy in the room. Which is good. You never want to be the smartest guy in the room or you are in the wrong room. Always be in a place to learn from others. But when the teacher in grade school would divide the class into the Lions, Tigers and Chipmunks, I knew, as well as my classmates knew, that as I took my seat with the Chipmunks, I was in the less likely to achieve group. My dear brother once told me that he and my parents would often talk about their low expectations for me. I told him that I knew where I was expected to fit in. I was never going to worry about being late for a Mensa Meeting. He went onto to explain in more detail the on-going concern he and my parent's had, for my poor chances in life. I had to assure him several times that I understood the dire chance for my future that people who knew me had for me. He continues to remind me what limited chance many people thought I had. I continue to tell him, "I know." When people see the projects, I have accomplished there is a surprised reaction and long explanations explaining their surprise. It's embarrassing, but not for me.

I have always thought if I can figure this economic stuff out so can anyone else. I have a few friends who have done very well economically and we talk sometimes about not doing well in school. They were often thought by others to be less likely to succeed and yet here we are with tremendous economic freedom. One friend confessed that when he is closing a big real estate deal and he has finished his part of the negotiation and the smart lawyers and accountants in the room start to discuss the complex contract points, he looks out the window and counts the leaves on the trees. He does not understand what they are saying and he does not care, he does not need to.

Say good bye to consumerism.

You could start this journey by becoming a lazy consumer. Too lazy to buy stuff you do not need. So here it is folks. Instead, grow your personal economy. Chances are you live in the 1 times 1 zone. You feel that you are never getting ahead financially because you are probably making poor economic choices every day. One important step to get you out of the 99% is to spend less then you make. Much propaganda is channeled to us every day to tell us to buy stuff. You deserve to treat yourself, get the six dollar cup of coffee. The only cell phone you can have is the most expensive one. What will people think if you have anything less. People don't see you in your house, they see you in your car. It must be a nice car. Forget this. I can drive a Porsche but I ride a thirty-five-dollar bike. I quit coffee because it keeps me up at night and I don't want to waste time making it or standing in a line for it. My phone cost a hundred dollars and I miss my free flip phone that I got free with my phone plan. Having money buys freedom from being under the thumb of anyone else but you. With economic freedom it is not what stuff you can buy it is the personal freedom you get in life. Stop buying crap that has no value after you buy it. Save your money and invest it. Crap is over rated. Most of what you buy is tomorrow's land fill. Make a budget and get interested in saving your money and then put your money to work for you. Send your money, like a good soldier, to fight for your economic freedom.

I got stuck in the bank the other day because the bank manager had to sign off on a transaction I was making. He saw what was in my bank account and after trying to convince me to work with one of the investment managers, which did not happen, he asked how I was so lucky. Lucky? He confessed that he wanted to do much better financially and he was a trained chartered accountant and had a business degree. He was a bright well-educated man. So why not? As I asked more questions of this young man and he described with great pride the choices he was making. He had bought a $100,000 car, an expensive house and lived an expensive disposable income lifestyle. No money left over to build an asset that went up in value, that could produce an income. He has all the ability and yet he did not make choices to match his aspirations.

I spend a lot of time in the incredible city of Havana Cuba. (I am writing this from my exceptional penthouse apartment on the ocean, which I under paid for and which has gone up in value by tens of thousands of dollars since I bought it.) Good for me. I can live here on a dollar a day. Every great city teaches you something. Havana has taught me that you do not need stuff. People live on twenty dollars a month. They are a communist country and they have not developed a consumer culture. There are no malls to hang out in. The few stores have very little to buy. People are not working in order to buy stuff they do not need or will end up in a rented storage compartment. There is no advertising here. What a relief. People spend time with friends and family instead of at work or shopping. We have been misinformed about what life's priorities are. People in Cuba rarely have debt. They do not have credit cards, lines of credit or mortgages. They have good education and health care. When things do not work, they make repairs, they do not throw stuff out. Cuba has economic issues but North America does to. We have too much debt for stuff we do not need and we do not invest in the infrastructure of our country and our people. Shame on us because we could have better economic health for our people and country. But we in North America can learn from Cuba. We do not need to buy stuff. We have been brain washed into thinking we have to buy buy buy. Consumer culture is stupid. Stop buying into it. Use your money to invest. Develop your friendships and family life. My bank manager guy who wanted to cross over to the 1% needs to sell his $100,000 car. He needs to be proud of his appreciating asset not his depreciating asset, which keeps him in the 99% for years to come. A $100,000 investment would be a rocket that jettisons him out of the 99%.

Look at your bank and credit card statements. Know your spending habits. What can you give up? Do you eat out too often? Buy too many shoes? Too many expensive gifts for others? Data plan too much? Sell your money sucking car.

With the money you save, invest it. But chose wisely. Invest like the 1%. You can invest in something that is very safe that is not likely to lose value or you can invest in things that go up in value quickly and make significant income. Also, when you get to a certain age say fifty-five to sixty, it is time to take less risk because it is harder to start over. But when you are young go for it. Take risk when you can start over. Learn from your mistakes and try again. Time has a profound effect on growing capital. It is more important how much time you have to invest rather than the amount. Five thousand invested over thirty years has a bigger pay out potential than fifty thousand for ten years.

Twenty some years ago I scraped together fourteen thousand dollars to put as a down payment on a house. I could have bought an okay car. My tenants over the years paid enough rent to cover the mortgage and they paid the utilities. The house became worth eight hundred thousand dollars. This was the best use of fourteen thousand dollars. The house was bought in an area that was considered not so good but it was within walking distance of the financial district of the city.

Multimillion dollar condo complexes have been built up all around the neighborhood to take advantage of the short walking distance to the banking district and a new subway link is going to be built in the neighborhood. The big kicker was when the property had $500,000 in equity, I borrowed this amount to buy another property which increased in value 1.5 million. That is putting money to work for you. That's the thinking of the 1%. This will not only make me wealthy but also my children and grandchildren wealthy. I wonder if they will thank me.

I was talking with a friend about his job and the misery of his work. John, my friend said his job was boring, same routine every day and he did not see any chance for improving. When I asked John what he wanted to do he said he would like to start his own business and work for himself, but he knew that this would require a great deal of money to start any business. Our mutual friend Tom was with us and he said some businesses when starting did not require hardly any more money than what most people have as a credit limit on a credit card. John shrugged this idea off. But Tom went on and explained that he wanted to invest in real estate, buy a rental property but no bank would lend him the money. Condos at the time were selling for $300,000. He did not have this much and it would take years to save this amount. No bank would lend him this amount based on his assets and income. But Tom met a private lender that explained another way to think about the situation. The private lender said that instead of the bank looking at Tom's assets and income the bank needed to see properties that were under-valued for similar properties in the area and generated an income greater than the property's expenses including the mortgage and utilities. Tom began to look at properties that were under-valued and produced more rental income than the mortgage payments and the tenant paid the utilities and property taxes. These properties were harder to find but worth it because they were the better business formula. The bank looked at the property's being under-valued as an asset and the rental income as the income to support the property. These factors were more important than Tom's assets and income.

John said this example only worked for property and did not apply to starting other businesses. Tom said that he knew a guy who wanted to start an import business of construction tools to a Caribbean country where there was a demand for power tools because the construction business was booming. Power tools that cost $100 at a hardware store in North American were selling for $400 in this Caribbean country. The cost of traveling to North America to get the tools would eat up most of the profit. But a courier delivery service was found that could get the required tools and delivery them for a reasonable price, in a timely way. The Caribbean guy just needed a credit card to place the order with the hardware store and arrange for the courier service to pick up and deliver the product. The cost was $100 a tool to start but left a profit of $300 a tool minus the deliver charge of $200 for ten tools. Ten tools made a profit of $2800. John said that was not that worth it. But Tom said it was the start of the business and it proved it was viable. In time with more orders the tool manufactures were approached directly and the tools were $35 each when bought in bulk and the delivery service, with an increase in business established an account and offered 60% off the delivery charges. Word spread among construction businesses that power tools could be bought at a reasonable rate and demand was good. This business stared with $1000.

John said that these were two good examples but most businesses needed large sums of money to start. Tom said he knew about a woman named Ruth who found a place that sold vegetarian roti for a dollar. She believed they were incredibly under-priced because they were so good and so filing that two of them were a whole meal. She found out that the store bought the roti for fifty cents and she was told which local restaurant was making them. She approached the restaurant and asked them to make an order of one hundred a day for two weeks. She found another store who agreed to sell them for $2.50 and the store would charge a dollar for each one they sold. The restaurant agreed to deliver the roti order each day. Ruth would pocket a dollar a roti. The roti were so good that they kept selling out. The order was increased to two hundred, the price went up to three dollars and another store agreed to sell the roti. Do the math. Learn the lesson.

John did not enjoy hearing about these three good examples from Tom and John told Tom to not be making up such crazy stories. Tom said John should pay for our drinks. What these stories explain are the road blocks some people have about the need for a lot of money to start a business. Business is about putting pieces together like a jig saw puzzle to create a whole picture. It is similar to a chemical formula that does what it needs to do. It involves risk, imagination and determination more than just money. Without a lot of money to start a business, it is a better formula because you are likely to make the best business decisions. If you have a great idea, and a good market, that formula is more important than money. The business should generate income easily and quickly and fuel development.

Money Money Money

Money is money. Profound. In a capitalistic culture money is everywhere and very available. It circulates all day every day and it is available to everyone. If you have a big pile of money good for you and use it wisely to invest in an asset that grows in value and creates an income. Do not invest more than you can afford to lose. Manage your risk. People are usually unrealistic about what they have. Some grossly under estimate what they have and some go completely the other way and overestimate their means. Everything that you own is an asset and can be sold or borrowed against to create an amount you can invest. Some people when they have a lot become very risk adverse and will not use any of their asset to invest in very safe ways. A friend with a three million dollar house, that is paid for, will not use any of the equity in his house to invest in an asset. Years ago, when I was broke a friend invited me to a fancy diner and everybody talked about their money worries. I began to realize these people were very well off and yet they worried about money. Having a lot of it does not stop you from worrying about money. Another friend who has no savings will borrow on his credit card to buy some inventory in order to sell it at a profit. The math seems to indicate that you have a good chance to make more but it will be your comfort with risk, your anxiety, fear and worry that will have a powerful impact on what you will finally do. Can you learn to control your anxiety because that would be helpful.

If you add up what you have and then find out what you can get as borrowed money, it is an important exercise. There are a number of sources of money. Here are some ideas. There are the big-name banks where can get loans and the types of loans have different names. But remember money is money. There are mortgages, which is a loan connected to a house. There are lines of credit and they may or may not be connected to an asset. There are credit cards which are not connected to any asset. The interest you pay on any of these loans changes dramatically, with the mortgage being the cheapest, next is the line of credit, and the most expensive loan, the credit card. Credit cards have a large range of interest charges, so shop around. Money is money but how much will it cost you to borrow the money. The more money you earn and the more money you have in an asset, the less it will cost you to borrow. That does not seem fair. When you are most in need with the least, it is harder and more expensive to get money. This is why people stay at zero sum gain economically. But it is another reason to become the 1%.

It is a game I used to play, how much can I get. I once, as a joke and as a game, I wanted to see if I could buy a property when I had no money as a down payment and the property was about five times more expensive than anything I had ever bought before. It was a great property but I truly believed it was out of my league. I had nothing to loss for trying. Nobody loves a coward. I was very surprised when the bank said YES. It scared me, it was outside of my usual by a lot. The building was a grand manor of a home, and it was a commercial and residential property. I had never done that before. But there was a Yes. I jumped, with fear, I jumped for the chance. It turned out to be a great deal.

Treat the hunt for money like a game. It is a bit complicated to know the many rules of how money is available and under what circumstances. But with a little bit of work most people can figure it out with great success. What holds most people back from getting start-up money is their own fear of risk, and their reluctance to seek out the money. It helps to have a really good idea and then people really want to get in on it.

It is good to eventually be your own bank, lending yourself money in a tax saving way. Seriously that is what you should be working for and our tax system completely favors the 1% and allows this. The interest on your loan goes to your beautiful self as an income and no longer goes to the bank. Understanding borrowing money is complex and the ways and rules regarding how you can borrow changes from place to place and the rules change over time. But the ways to borrow money is a study in itself and can be a body of knowledge that could be one of your most important tools to getting where you want to go to build yourself financially. It does not cost anything to go to different banks and find out what you are eligible for. But go to several different banks because the rules change from institution to institution. And there are different levels of banks. There are banks with a name brand. They have many branches and many strict rules about who and how they lend. There are the second tare banks, credit unions, trust companies etc. smaller institutions, less restrictions to lend money. There are private lenders who have extra cash and want to lend their money in a contractual way to an investment they think is safe.

Here is a “concept” about money that I hope is useful.

One times -One= -1
One times One = 1
two times two= 4 better
four times four= 16 very good
sixteen times sixteen =132 now we are talking 1%

1 times -1 Many people spend more money than they make. Every day the things you buy cost more money than you make. You are programed through advertising to spend. The way you spend is made more convenient and rewarded. You can “tap” your way to happiness and get ‘rewards’ as you go. At the end of every day, week, month, year, you are more and more in debt and many consumer goods do not appreciate in value. The consumer goods you buy are the easiest to get debt money for through credit cards and this is the most expensive money. There is great knowledge that I call “evil phycology” that has been developed to get you to spend on stuff you do not need, you cannot afford and drives you into debt. You have been sucked in to consumer spending debt.

1 times 1 Most people live economically at one times one. What you make is what you spend. You have nothing left over. Nothing. This means you have nothing to invest. You cover your cost of living, rent and food, some entertainment, and cloths. You can spend what you make at any income level. Entertainers or professional athletes have often spent everything they have made and when their career ends, they have little to show for the money they earned. Many with a middle-class income spend as they go and in their fifties as people around them retire, they realize they have no investment to provide an income for when they are not

working. Some ignore the consumer culture message. There is much less investment information given to you. If you invest your money the money goes to work for you. The money if invested wisely grows an income and an asset. Some investments do not grow. My very intelligent accomplished neighbor told me she invested $100,000 fifteen years ago and the investment is now worth $105,000. With inflation factored in, she lost money. That's embarrassing. This is a story of one times one. She did not check on the investment to see if it was generating an income or growing as an asset. Very embarrassing. At least her investment did not lose money which of course is possible.

2 times 2. Some people live somewhat below their income. Instead of buying a $30,000 car, which the bank will let them finance, they get a $20,000 car. The difference in payments, they invest. They make coffee at home and do not get the designer coffee with a leaf imprint in the foam for five dollars and an organic gluten free muffin for four dollars. At twenty work days a month, they save $180 a month. Instead of spending they invest. They go to the scratch and dent room first at the furniture store and pay 60% off of the full price. They have an automatic saving plan at work that takes off 10% of their income and puts it into a tax-free investment plan. They are saving for their future with little effort or risk and over time they grow a good investment.

4 times 4. At this level you climb the economic ladder. You complete more education and improve your chances for higher paying jobs. You develop an investment and make responsible choices to grow it as an asset and income producer. You develop more of your ability to earn an income with some knowledge of investments. You pay down your mortgage and try to pay off credit cards and develop a saving and investment plan. You are living below your means especially when you are young and investing and using time to create wealth. Some friends in their late twenties after getting their first real job with an okay income, qualified for a

great big car loan and bought a beautiful car that reflected who they were as an individual. Their depreciating asset was fun to drive and after four years it was worth a fraction of what they paid for it. Others bought an under-valued house in an up-and-coming neighborhood. Different paths were chosen. Ten years later the house tripled in value. They had paid down their mortgage and had started investing in the stock market.

At this level you are living a good middle class life. You are living below your means and the left-over money you are investing, usually in aggressive investments that are likely going to give you an income that will help support you when you are older and not working. Safe predictable reasonable responsible 99% thinking. Vanilla with a dash of chocolate. But you picked up a book about the 1%. Are you not curious about what are the bigger possibilities?

16 times 16. This is living and thinking like the 1%. Watch out. Here we go. Get out of my way. You are going over the 'wall'. You are not dependent on any employer, bank or spouse, parent or anyone else for your economy. You are in control of how and what you work at. Part of it is you have enough money or assets and income that gives you financial freedom. You are not beholding or dependent on anyone else to provide for you. You have 'your freedom money.' Instead of being dependent on an employer for your source of income you have developed an accumulating asset builder and income generator that YOU have created. Some buy lottery tickets waiting for the pay off. But what if you had the knowledge to create your own economy. This knowledge is more important than the money. What if you lived in the passing lane of life financially?

This level of functioning is only partly to do with how much you have. At this level of finances, you are easily able to pay your daily living costs with lots left over. You have money left to invest. But at this level you have economic freedom. Your income is from a resource outside of your daily efforts. Your income comes from a source that is less dependent on you. This frees you. An example is a rental property. Your tenant needs to work to earn the money to pay you for the use of the property. The rental property needs to keep providing shelter to earn the income to be transferred to you. The mortgage on the property is paid off and you borrow on the property's equity to invest in more income producing and asset building investments. Or the store you own and its products, need to keep functioning to provide you with an income. Or the device you invented needs to continue to provide a use for people to want it, buy it and give you an income. Don't you wish you had invented the light bulb?

There is a great podcast called "How I Built This." It is an interview with entrepreneurs and their story of how they developed their business. Their problems, their failures and their successes. What they learned along the way. Learn these lessons to own your own economy at the level that makes sense to you. Get where you want to go and be what you want to be.

At this level you are working to develop income generators and asset builders to support you. You look outside yourself for financial generators. There are few people in the world that through their daily work for others earn a great income. And your job is not an asset and it is not an asset that grows in value. If your company rewards you with stock in the company and the company does well you are building an asset but this is a rare experience. A great asset gains value over time and produces an income. The 1% get this knowledge. The 1% realize that income producing asset builders are the priority. The 99% focus on an income. You are limited to what you can earn at a job. Most jobs, no matter how talented you are or how hard you work, you get paid what you get paid and one day you will not work. How will you support yourself? An asset can support you in your old age and an asset is what you leave to your children. You cannot leave them a job. But you can leave them an asset that produces an income. There are many inventions, businesses, income producing properties that generate income and assets. You want to grow a money-making tree. Create a money machine. You want the money machine to work to earn the income to pay to you. This gives you freedom. The holy grail of wealth. Stuff you buy in a store, to some is the symbol of wealth, but assets that increase in value and provide on-going income, giving you economic freedom and frees up your time. This is a more profound symbol of wealth.

Exercise

Figure out what level you are at:
1--1 1-1 2-2 4-4 16-16
Decide what level you want to be.
List your resources that will help you get to where you want to go.
Include in your resources your beautiful self. What is it about you that will get you where you want to go? Work ethic, resilience, intelligence, creativity, education, open mindedness, untapped resources in yourself or in your life.

Go to where the 1% are. Go to where they shop, go for coffee, diner, the park they walk their dog. Go and take in what they do, who they are, the choices they make.

The 1% get to be more of their own person. March to their own drum. Be more id. They do not have to conform to a boss, corporate culture, opinion of coworkers. They do not have to fit in. They are free to be who they are without "filters." Often the 1% are said to be eccentric which is a more polite way to say crazy and rich. Sometimes their behaviors do not make sense to anyone, but themselves because they do not need to. As part of the 1% you will more likely be judged but you do not have to care because you are not economically dependent.

The 1% spend less time doing grunt work. Activities that are of low intellect, or creativity and boring. They have more time and energy to do more interesting, self-fulfilling energizing endeavors which is good for them psychologically and for productivity. Try it for a week no grunt work. See what you get up to.

I like to go to the upper east side of Manhattan, a hot bed of the 1% of the 1%. The show is breathtaking. Some of the eccentric ways are hilarious to watch play out. People are so free economically they follow their own rules. People who have had their hair, and their dog's hair-cut, styled and colored the same as their own. It is said that people look like their pets. You make this dream come true on the upper east side. These people never hail their own cabs, that is what a doorman does. And they never leave the building till the cab is out front and ready for you. A woman never carries her purse out of the building to the cab. The doorman does that. Once in the cab the doorman hands the lady her purse and closes the cab door. This is the 1% avoiding any grunt work to the extreme. But more so the 1% are a pampered protected, catered to group. Over years of this specialized treatment, you would have a higher sense of entitlement. You would naturally make choices for the best opportunities to keep you in this rarified world. This is where the 1% think and make choices differently than the 99%. The 1% have different expectations. They see themselves at the front of the line with the best service. Where do you put yourself, what are your expectations?

Many books have been written about the life of the people of the upper east side and the fascinating things they get up to. What you want to find out is what is the priorities of the 1%, what choices do they get to make that the 99% don't get to make, what do they value? But find your own 1% and find your own way to observe and learn from them. Join an investor group, yes even when you have no money. You are on a mission to learn. Develop your version of the question "What does the 1% know that you do not know?"

The crazy observations of the 1% are very entertaining. I believe that your quest to becoming the 1% should be an adventure and make it an entertaining adventure. Yes this is work but it can be engaging and fascinating which is good for your motivation.

What I see for the 1% is the choices they have, to live a life with more freedom and the power to influence their environment. They live in a very protected, rarified way. There is a street in the upper east side of Manhattan called Park Avenue. The people living on this street live the life of the 1%. You live with a great deal of protection where you have a buffer from the realities of the world. Your doorman greets you when you come home and says good-bye to you when you leave. You are welcomed and protected as you should be, every day. You are the 1%. Having a Park Avenue address is coveted because it is influential. When you say that you live on "Park" many people allow you access to situations that the 99% are not allowed to enter. One block away from this address, living in the same amount of space is not only a fraction of the price but more importantly has no credentials, comes with no invitation.

I was once at an open house to a Park Avenue apartment. A very small, 400 square foot apartment, badly laid out with some gaudy finishes. Two million dollars was the price. The same size apartment one block away was for sale for $300,000. They were both made of bricks and mortar. The overly botoxed real estate agent approached me and asked where I was currently residing. I gave her the address of the apartment, which was several blocks away. She recoiled as though I was unclean, a desperate vagrant from the street. She pointed to me and said "I have never been over there." She dismissed me and walked away. The other people attending the open house were residences of the building.

They were interested in the apartment to use as either storage, an office or a place for the maid to stay but the space was valuable to them because it was close to their apartment in the building. Oh, the incredible luxury of choice. Two million for a place to keep the ski equipment, off season.

What I have learned from my passive observation of the very rich is, they have a freedom that most do not know was possible. They put a value on things that most do not know are so valuable. Time is more valuable than the 99% know. We all have the same time each day but the rich pay heavily to not waste time. The time they would save to have a second place in the same apartment building as their home apartment, is very important. The super convenience to eliminate the travel time to get to a private office, because it is in the same building is valuable. Some apartment buildings have the garage parking for their car in the apartment itself. There is a special elevator to take their car to their apartment, which may be on the twenty third floor. This is super convenient and saves time. The parking spot costs a million dollars for that luxury. Time is money.

I do not want to live on Park Avenue. There are many rules a person has to follow to show that they are truly part of the micro culture of this street. I am not interested in proving anything to this group and they do not care if I do. Thank you I am busy. But I am grateful and amused by what I have learned from this group and its application to my own life has been very helpful. I knew I had learned about time from the 1% when I was out with my friend Alice and we were having trouble finding parking. I parked in a place that I would likely get an expensive parking ticket but I took the available spot any way. It would have taken too much time to find available parking. Alice was upset and said that I was going to get the ticket and how could I be so foolish. I tried to explain that the time saved was completely worth the ticket. She had trouble accepting this idea. When she saw the ticket on the car when we returned to the parking spot, she said she had warned me.

But what really bothered her was seeing that the costly ticket had no meaning to me. The value of time had meaning. Thank you, Park Avenue. Priorities of the 1%.

The 1% have the luxury of nurturing themselves at a higher level. They have the time and the means to put themselves in situations to learn from the most knowledgeable sources, to create a space where they can be creative with limited restraint and take risk with new opportunities. For example, a 1% person can more easily have the time and means to develop a new idea or be in a situation to hear about a new technology break through. They have the means to develop a start-up company and take the risk to make an investment.

Make a space

What can you learn from this as a 99% person? You go to work each day and your most productive time and greatest energy, goes to working for someone else. You are a cog in the wheel with some financial reward for yourself, your income. You have limited time and energy left over for something you create for your own financial benefit. Something you create that has the potential to grow in value and income. Think about the union rules regarding pay increases. It is based on time, not talent, or productivity, or capital gain for the institution that you are building. Think about words like pay grid, seniority, these are the artificial restrictions on what you can possibly earn. These restrictions even things out. The less productive and people with limited talent are put even with the hardest workers with the most talent. The work environment you create when you work for yourself has no artificial restrictions. Usually the harder you work, and the more talent you have, the more valuable the asset you are creating becomes. Think about it. But the problem is time and energy to create something that is yours, something with no limits. You need to find a crack in your time, to plant a seed that can grow with nutrients into something that has a life of its own. And you must find this time and you must protect it from the competing demands. Once time has passed it is gone forever. It is like the hotel business. If you do not rent the room out tonight that chance to rent it out is gone, you cannot go back in time to capture that opportunity. If you truly believe in your project create a place in your life for it to happen. Seriously consider your priority in this matter. If your effort and time dedicated to the project is low the results will show. If you just squeeze a little bit of time at the end of the day, when you are tired this will be reflected in your results. I talked with a lovely woman a while ago who explained that she spent ten years writing her book, it was obviously not a priority. For ten years she sometimes worked on her book.

Consider what time you put into grunt work, managing your home and watching tv, surfing the net, social media, shopping. Also consider your time with family, friends and work. What do you do for others that they could do for themselves and you are resentful for doing. At work do you arrive early and leave late and do work for several other coworkers staying late to finish up what others did not think was important to do. Stand down good citizen. What would it be like to put that time and effort into your own project. How wicked and selfish would you be? You need to cut some of your obligations and have an obligation to yourself and what you are creating. This can be a profound shift in your understanding of how you fit with the people in your life. But it is a great shift in psychology and the way of life you have been programed to follow as a 99% person. A change from working for others to working for yourself is a great shift in sensibility. The middle-class mentality has many positives but you need to free yourself from the draw backs. If you stay in the mind-set of a middle-class person, you will not grow an asset that will support yourself or your family. You will just be an average wage earner. You will be subject to the highest tax, and not eligible for the greatest tax advantages. It is not what you earn it is what you keep. You will never get out from under the limits of your limited financial circumstances. You will not find financial freedom.

Make the project a "thing." A place you go, an activity you fall into. You are creating a new mindset. You are developing something important, something new and special. You are on an adventure. Get into it and enjoy it. Make it dynamic, compelling and exciting. This project is to stretch you, it is going to be hard and so it helps that the project is breathtakingly engaging and gives to your spirit. You want to be hungry to do it and passionate about it. You are making a dream come true.

Alice

Alice is a very intelligent hard worker and a slave to the 99% doctrine. She has often arrived early for work and not only been diligent about doing her work but helped many others do their job even if it meant she stayed late and worked the odd weekend. Few coworkers ever put in as much time as she did. What time she had outside of work she worked hard around her modest home to keep it bright and clean. She was very generous with her children helping them out of financial tight spots when they could not make ends meet. She drives a car that is beyond her financial means. The expensive car was her last chance to feel that she is part of a wealthier life. Alice knows when she finishes work in a few years she may not be able to even afford a car. It will be the bus for her so she is going to enjoy this pricy car while she can. It is her last chance to see herself in the life she imaged for herself and to have others see her as a well-off person. She sits on a great deal of anger regarding her lot in life. She knows that she is bright and hardworking but she is aware that others of less intelligence and work ethic have so much more freedom economically than she does. At age sixty-one she sees many friends and family members retiring, traveling the world, deciding what to do rather than fulfilling employment obligations. She is tired. Alice wants to be done with the day-to -day work demands, but financially she knows she cannot. She is bitter because she sees where people's spouses help create financial independence while she had two spouses that took part of her financial assets. Alice hears how people through long term investments are quite impressed with the large financial nest egg they have created and the choices they get to have. She is very aware of the bad choices she made that left her with practically no nest egg and she has fear that when work ends, her economic life will be limited. At the most vulnerable time in her life, she will not be middle class with a modest home and a car. She will slip into poverty. She will have enough to eat and she will need to rent a modest apartment but the extras in life as a middle-class person will slip away. She is bitter and afraid. She is also ashamed at how this happened to her. She thought she could expect more out of life. And if she sees one more commercial about a happy care free senior skipping through Tuscany she is going to lose it.

You can learn from the 1% how they buy time. What can you do that cheats time? The 99% do a lot of grunt work. How much grunt work do you do? Grunt work is work far below your skill level, but you do it anyway. The 99% waste a great deal of time producing things of no real value to themselves. You may be a great employee but how good are you as an employee to yourself. Examine your time. Do you have a super clean house? Could you eat off the floor. Do you not have plates and a table? How is it valuable to eat off a floor when that time and energy can be used to develop a product or a business to serve you? You need to create a space in your time for your development. Too much time shopping on line, commuting, cleaning. What will you give up to have time to create opportunities for yourself? There are a lot of norms set for the 99% that without a lot of thought the 99% follow. Norms that suck a lot of time and energy out of your life. I used to associate with people who spent a lot of time, money and energy having the cleanest driveway and the most perfect lawn. Hours every night and weekend pulling weeds, fertilizing, cutting grass so they could impress their neighbors with golf course putting green, grade lawns. This was some norm that made sense to them. Also washing their driveways. Clean enough to eat off of. Treating the asphalt with special chemical sealants. A chemical warfare with the asphalt that held no bounds. What boundaries will you put in place to provide a place to do something very important for yourself, that you own, that gives back to you. Look at your efforts and how they benefit you.

If you spend not just your time, but your energy giving to your day job how will you have nothing left over for what you create. It helps to get interested in something you are passionate about. Something that matters to you, creates a "fire in your belly." Something that intrigues you, that you cannot get enough of. Something that you are addicted to. It is not work for you, it is a joy. Maybe it should be a lawn care service or driveway servicing business. Take what you know, what you are curious about and expand. Your obsessive quirk could be something you develop into your business. You feel tired at the end of the day, but you feel energized when you dive into what you are interested in. Many people spend more time suppressing what they have a passion for then developing it.

Exercise

Make a list of your grunt work. Work that you wish you could give to someone else.
Question the value of the time and effort you put into this grunt work. Do you value this work or is it for someone else?
Measure the time you put into your grunt work.
Decide in a cost benefit kind of way what you would find as a more beneficial way to spend your time and energy.
What would you rather be doing?

Do these activities suck the life out of you?

Interests

What are your hobbies, what are you interested in?
What are you passionate about?
What do you seek information about?
Rate your enjoyment factor.
Find the energy that is already within you. And release it and grow it directly into an asset that will grow for you.

Ways people become the 1%

Jane worked for an investment firm. She got hired as a secretary and assistant to a junior financial analyst. Jane had a great work ethic she did her job and she did more. She saw the missing pieces in how the investment house worked and she completed the gaps. Jane eventually reorganized the firm from the ground up and made it work in a seamless way that the partners in the firm did not know was possible. The partners began to realize how valuable Jane was and wanted to reward all that she had done for them. They met with Jane and gave her a good pay raise but purposed to her to take her on as a client and help her invest her money. Usually, their clients had to have one million in assets or they would not take an interest. Jane was not familiar with investing but she had respect for what the partners were doing because she heard the client's feed-back about what great work they did. She decided to give them a try for a year. Jane was very careful about her money and had saved a great deal. After seeing good results with her investments Jane gave over half of her savings. When she retired, she had more than the required one million in her investment account.

It is possible to become a savvy investor in the stock market. It is important to do your research and understand how the market works. You may find a good financial planner, but you need to know how the market works and tax implications. If you totally rely on a financial planner, you are making a huge mistake. First, you are not growing anything about yourself or your knowledge, or your ability to deal with risk. Growing economically is a great chance to grow as a person. Develop extra skills and knowledge. You are also too open to risk if you just leave your money in one person's hands without your having knowledge to supervise what they are doing. One friend got stuck with mutual funds that their financial advisor was asked to unload by the bank they worked for. While the market went up these poorly performing mutual funds slowly but steadily lost money and they were charged a percentage of the capital for managing the investment. Ouch. You need to know and take responsibility for your investments.

Don't quit your day job kind of investments can up your risk but are demanding for your time when you start them up. Many business ideas with extra work can be limited in their need for your day-to-day involvement. A friend named Fred bought a ten acre farm and cleared the land and had crops grown specifically for several restaurants. The start-up work was demanding but he designed the working of the farm and the interaction with the restaurants to work seamlessly. Eventually there was limited input needed from him so he was free to develop other businesses. Fred explained to me that he saw the need from restaurants to have a steady reliable source of fresh food specific to their needs and the restaurant staff picked up of the vegetables from the farm. He had always wanted to own a farm and grow vegetables and have a few chickens and goats. He had an interest in growing plants and an ongoing need to know more about farming. Fred found some people who wanted to live in the country and he could offer them a place to live and access to the food they grew in exchange for managing the growing of the required crops. He was building a supply chain. Once the links of the chain were in place, he was able to be fairly free. He just added new information about growing crops from time to time and just checked to see if the links in the chain were strong and working together.

Another friend always wanted a store, but she had no time to be in the store everyday selling her specialty items. But she had a friend who had worked retail years ago and liked the experience but did not want to work for someone else. They agreed to be partners. With combined income and assets, they qualified to buy a small commercial space in a retail mall. The friend that kept her day job was responsible for sourcing the supple of their product and the friend managed the day-to-day operation of the store. They worked well together and looked at expanding to a second space with another product.

There are great opportunities with online sales. This is a world onto itself and it looks like it is taking over from bricks and mortar retail. There are so many possibilities and great stories about how people have found a great product and learned to position it on the internet in such a way that what they are selling goes to the front of the line, because it is a great product and they have a great way for it to get attention. To develop a supply chain that is reliable is key to this working. The competition is fierce and this is good because it will bring out your best efforts. The book Boss Girl is a good read about how online marketing, if done well has great rewards. Good Luck

There is also real estate. Rental property once it is up and running can supply an ongoing income and the chance for capital appreciation. People always say how expensive real estate is and it is impossible to invest in. I worked with a woman who was about sixty years of age and she managed a property eight hours drive away. She worked hard to have the most reliable mechanics in the house, the furnace, electrical and plumbing systems. She kept a list of local people to manage any problems that occurred. She was a little crazy. She would put a ladder on the roof of her car, and a lawn mower in her trunk and drive the eight hours to fix an eve trough and cut the lawn. She liked the house, it was very charming, a “one off” New England salt box. She found a house she could afford and the problem was it was eight hours away, but she made it work. I was so inspired by her example I found two houses built on one lot, beautiful homes, fireplaces, gables and dormers, sliding pocket doors, an attic left empty for me to use as I needed through a private back staircase. The two houses cost $40,000 and made $2000 a month in rent. Figure out what the mortgage is on $40,000. I used a line of credit to buy these beautiful homes. Months would go by when all I did was cash rent cheques and I had the tenant cut the lawn and shovel the snow.

Bob the neighbor

My neighbor up the street who has one of the nicest homes in the neighborhood will turn the garden hose on you when you walk past his house. He will yell at you as he sprays you. “Keep moving freak you are lowering my property values.” I like this guy. He is pure id. He has no constraints on what he says and does. He is pure impulse. No filters. Bob not only has the nicest house in the neighborhood but he owns several commercial properties in the area. He does not need to work. He is not obligated to anyone for his income or way of life. Bob is free to say and do what he wants.

Talking with Bob is always an adventure and a learning experience. I noticed years ago if I talked about some pitiful obligation, I thought I had at work or in my life Bob would look at me with a grimace and say “why would you do that, are you stupid?” Bob is the 1%. He controls his own time, determines his own agenda, owes nothing to know body. He is a very free man to do what he wants, when he wants to and he does. He looks at the activities of the 99% and laughs. Bob has a perspective that seems arrogant and dismissive, because it is. But more profound he sees what the 99% are doing and interprets their activities solely from his position of the 1%. He does not apologize for what he is or what he has. He has freedom in our culture that comes from economic freedom. He is not constrained to fit into a corporate structure day after day. He has not adapted himself to be with others at work or in the neighborhood. Bob has the luxury of choice. To speak his mind with no concern for consequences. The luxury of standing on your own with no obligation to adapt himself to others. Wouldn't it be nice?

Over the years I have created a life outside of the 99%. Bob still questions what I am doing but with curiosity not disdain. He still will turn the garden hose on me and I would be disappointed if he didn't.

One of the saddest things was watching a coworker named Ellen, who over the years went from being part of the 1% to the 99%. My coworker was extremely good at her job. Highly affective, hard worker, very respected. She only worked part time. She did not need to work because her husband made a lot of money, until he didn't. She said she only worked to get away from her children, who she loved but who drove her crazy. Ellen said what she wanted. She spoke a truth to management that only a person can say when they have no fear of losing their job. She would say crazy things. "How do you work full time, when would you get your nails done?" She used to bring the world's largest emery board (It was the size of a skate board and it probably had wheels) to staff meetings and file her nails. If Ellen wanted to make a point, she would rap the emery board on the metal arm rests of the chair to get every one's attention. And then she would speak her opinion. It kept you on the edge of your seat.

But when her husband lost his giant income and the big house had to go and private school was no longer possible for the kids, Ellen had to work full time, she got afraid and she got quiet. That scared the rest of us. What was happening to her? It told the rest of us how afraid we were. It was not just that Ellen was an opinionated free spirit who spoke her mind. She felt safe due to economic freedom to have an opinion and express it. Were we all squeezed because we were too afraid for our jobs? Yes. We stayed quiet not in a deliberate way.

We just knew instinctively that it was necessary in order to be secure that we had to go with the flow. It was hard to be with someone who had to change from being free to someone who had to contain themselves like the rest of us. At least for a while. Either way it was a reflection of how constrained we all were. How dependent and stifled.

Who do you think you are? How you define yourself is part of how you stay in the 99%

The house I grew up in was always referred to as Izzie Bordon's house. Although my parents paid cash and lived in the house for thirty-five years the house was known as Izzie's house. I remember our neighbor talking to my father about his choice of paint for the house's back steps. My father who was color blind choose a color the same used for the town's fire engine, (he probably found it in the mistake paint section and thought it was a lively gray.). My neighbor with a critical tone said to my dad "Izzie would not have used that color!" My dad said "well of course not because, Izzie is dead." Friendly small town.

In my town your house was not ours, it was the previous owner's house. I don't know why and nobody else knew why, either. You were not your own unique self either. My Dad's name was Brock and I was always Brock's son. Probably many did not know I had a name, I was just Brock's son. Who I was, my lot in life, why or how I did anything was filtered through being Brock's son? "Why did that kid drive through town so fast?" "Well, because he is Brock's son." It would not be because I was drunk and joy riding. No that wasn't it, ever.

How much of how you think of yourself is up to you? How you think of yourself is often filtered through what you have been told about yourself from your family, friends and at school. Some of it was accurate, some of it made sense when you were a kid and some of it was manipulation to get you to behave in a certain way. How you think of yourself also comes from the culture you are raised in, your religion and the media, especially advertising.

However, you define yourself, where ever the ideas about yourself came from you are probably more loyal to this definition then you realize. People, even when they do not like some ways about their character and behavior hang onto it because it is familiar. It helps you decide where you should be and what you should be doing even if it is a bad place with few good out comes. Breaking out of how you define yourself is very hard for most people. If you think of yourself as part of the 99%, as most do, you are going to resist breaking into the 1%. It is not familiar, but more to the point it is not you, it is not how you think of yourself and it is not how anyone else thinks of you. But what if it is time to open up, think of new ideas, see what is possible for your abilities, opportunities in life. What if you could be more of your own person on your own terms and not be in the shadow of those before you, or who surround you now. What if you gave yourself a big chance in life and lived by your own definition of yourself and your circumstances.

Roadblocks

What stands in your way of what you want in life? There are real limitations in life around time, opportunity, environment, your abilities, but there are the roadblocks you put in your own way that you could begin to examine and root out and push away. How do you hold yourself back from what you want, what you could be?

There are the people in your life that will try to contain you. They know who you are and it will be important to them that you stay inside that definition. It will bother them if you try and become different from what they think you are. People get anxious about people and situations that change and a lot of people like predictability. If they think you are getting better than them, some take it as a threat. There will be some that may be supportive and even help you. Other people and their opinions can seem like road blocks to your trying to be more and have more opportunity or not. It will be up to you to see how much of other people's opinion you will absorb or how much you will shake off.

The biggest consideration for roadblocks will be you. Yes, go look in the mirror and see what you see. Yes, it is you staring back at yourself. The good news is you do not have to wait for someone else or circumstances outside of yourself to change or cooperate or anything else. It comes down to you. You have immediate access to yourself. You can influence yourself. But often people have psychological roadblocks regarding influencing themselves, controlling themselves, following their own agenda. Getting to know how you hold yourself back, how you have an ongoing internal fight between what you want and stop yourself from achieving these goals, is an important piece of psychological work. If you clean out your internal bureaucracy, image how smooth your life could be. How peaceful. In developing your best relationship with yourself, where you have the most self-respect, confidence and good will with yourself is important for good psychological health. When you get rid of the roadblocks that get in your way of what you want for yourself it is a major step in a good relationship with yourself. If you watch yourself accomplish important goals in your life, provide for yourself in a meaningful way, even accede your expectations, develop yourself to your full potential learn and grow as a person, you are likely to develop a powerful belief in yourself. Also known as self-confidence.

Some of the roadblocks people have are what you allow yourself to do, be a part of. I am interested in the design of spaces and some of the best examples of great design is in fancy store interiors. Top name brand stores have huge budgets to create exceptional interior space. I am surprised when a number of friends refuse to enter top name brand stores.

They say "they do not want me in their store. I don't belong in there. I cannot afford anything in that place."

How often do you hold yourself back from being with people, being in places that you think are beyond your "place" in life? That is your bureaucracy. Crossing a threshold into a high name brand store is not physically impossible experience but it can seem like a psychological impossibility unless you work through this issue.

Perfectionistic behavior can be seen as having high standards or a very complicated way to get anything done. If you have a rigid controlling nature this is a piece of internal bureaucracy that may get you some reward somewhere in your life but can cause great problems in your relationships with others and makes it very complicated to get anything accomplished. These are your "too many rules", too many complex complications that are roadblocks to getting stuff done. They are your rules, your complications dial it down. It is just anxiety, fear and worry that is being dysfunctionally managed through perfectionism. Handling real risk as you venture forward will bring your unresolved anxiety forward. Deal with it or not. But it is your anxiety to work through and do not put this onto someone else or circumstances to change. Your anxiety is your anxiety. What are you going to do about it?

Some of the roadblocks that keep people in the 99% are things that can be learned or worked through psychologically.

Some of the issues are fear of responsibility. People are afraid of criticism that comes with responsibility. If you are in charge, you are open to the blame if you get it wrong. Some people are phobic about criticism and will avoid it at all costs. If you have a poor relationship with yourself, if you do not like yourself and believe that you are inadequate you probably do not want to be vulnerable to other's criticism of you. You are already an open wound psychologically because of your painful relationship with yourself. If you have not developed a positive self-image, you will be too open to the negative criticism from others. You will not have developed a thick skin or psychological defense mechanisms to keep out other's negative opinions.

If you avoid responsibility, you avoid the glory that comes with the success of what you take charge of. This is a great source of self-confidence. You feel good about yourself when you create something and you realize its success you earn self-esteem points. Avoiding responsibility is not good for your sense of competence. You can learn to cope with criticism. Separate yourself out from criticism. "What I did, did not work out, I am still a good person. I can learn from my mistakes." Making mistakes is part of trying, learning.

You can learn leadership skills. Improve your communication skills. Become more assertive, say what you want directly to people. Ask for help, tell people your expectations of them, proved constructive criticism. Leadership skills help you be more effective with others. Most people feel better about themselves if they develop leadership skills. Develop trust with others by following through with what you say you are going to do.

People do not take on responsibility because they have not grown up psychologically. They still want to be taken care of by someone else. They still want to be parented. But what they are missing is the joy of being independent not having to be under the rules of someone else and the restrains of dependence. You have to give up or never grow your own agenda if you stay dependent on someone else financially, like an employer, spouse, parent.

Some people carry in their thoughts an internal dialogue of worry, fear and guilt. Whatever they do they filter it through thoughts of worry, fear and guilt. This slows them down and helps talk themselves out of many opportunities. “I would like to try starting my own business but what if...impending doom, disaster, fire and flood... Learning to realistically interpret situations is important and learning self-soothing messages are important.

Exercise

Go to the cheapest store that sells notepads and buy one. Write out your roadblocks as they present themselves to you. “I want to have more assets and income and my roadblocks are... Leave room under each roadblock to describe how you will overcome this roadblock and move on because you are on the move with other issues to overcome. Own the roadblock, kick down the roadblock.

Risk. The biggest risk is not to take one, especially when you have nothing.

I believe people can change their lot in life. Recently I ran into a friend I had not seen in thirty years. He did not seem to have changed at all. I show the signs of my age and yet he recognized me. When I knew Bruce thirty years ago, he was an important executive able to bring together very complex people and resource for tremendous success. He was the producer of Broadway style theater and he was just thirty years old. He was very smart, arrogant in a lovable way and he had a bravado that I had never seen before. I felt so very fortunate that we became friends. I always wondered why he gave me the time of day I was living a small life with seemingly little chance for more. I would tell Bruce my day dream of buying a house and fixing it up. He gave me a fancy book by one of the best interior design gurus of the time, a very expensive, very informative book and he wrote a beautiful note wishing me well in pursuing my dream. I did not know that a book just dedicated to design ideas could exist. It was a body of knowledge that I did not know people thought about or would make an entire book about. Each page was an eyeful of spectacular pictures and informative text about the knowledge of design. The book had ideas taken from the best homes from all over the world and through different eras of time. The book changed my life for two reasons. The belief and encouragement from my friend that my dream was possible. That meant a great deal to me. I had great respect for his knowledge and ability. I took what he said to heart and grew the idea of what I would do. The book he gave me opened up a body of knowledge that has served me well for many years. I looked through that book taking in every picture, every concept, every idea and I began a quest for more books and knowledge regarding architecture and interior design. The book was the spark to a passion I barely knew I had. It was amazing to see my friend again after thirty years. We got together and I showed him the book he gave me with worn pages and I showed him his tender encouraging words that he wrote thirty years ago that started a great journey for me.

We got together in a home I had just finished building. The house was a true culmination of everything I had learned about design over the years. It was a small house and a place to practice many design features. The house did not offer size it could only offer aesthetic. I used every design feature I could think of. I opened the home up to have the best use of light. As the sun moved around the home during the day the windows were positioned to take in the sun. Attention to the movement of shadow in the house was important so it was as though the home was alive with an ever-changing pattern and light using direct light and shadow so the home seemed ever changing and alive. Rooms could be dramatically altered because walls could move to change their use and size as the owner required. The most exquisite tile, wood, and colored glass, were used to add a sense of luxury to the space. The house was small but the rooms were large to always give the sense of great space. High ceilings, long views added to a sense of space. A light box lit by skylights was positioned in the center of the home, punctuated by the stairs which were designed as a sculpture. This was a main feature. When I met Bruce, he had a beautiful apartment filled with found treasures from his world travels and I had a small, dingy apartment in the city's ghetto neighborhood with a photon I had found on the street and a lamp. It was very meaningful to have my friend, after all these years with his critical eye, see what I had created and hear his comments.

I always thought the biggest risk is not to take one. I came from nothing. In my early twenties I had a job that did not pay enough to cover rent and food. Every month I got further behind. One Christmas I had no money for presents, which was good because I had no money to go home to my parent's home. But these problems were solved when I found a couple of twenty-dollar bills swirling in the wind two days before Christmas Day. I had nothing to lose to take risks and try and get ahead financially. I first invested in more education so I could get a job that paid better. I got a loan to pay for school and I worked while I went to school. It was a risk to take on the education debt and invest the time in a degree that hopefully would lead to a job with more income. All of these hopes came true. Better job, more income. I eventually earned enough to afford food and rent. Hora! I was living the dream. But I had felt the fear of getting close to homelessness. I did not just want to exist (one times one) I wanted some economic security. (Two times two) I got a second job. I worked as a waiter in the evening after my day job ended. I had no time to spend money and I lived off my waiter tips and saved my income from my day job. I found a friend who also wanted to get ahead financially and we bought an ugly house in a bad neighborhood. The house did not even have a bathroom. I became a frequent patron of the neighborhood fast food place for my bathroom needs. This was risky, buying a house that was in such bad shape. I knew nothing about renovations and had little money to pay for renovations. My friend knew of a plumber who said he would work for cigarettes because he wanted to get away from his nagging wife and he was blind and no one wanted to hire him. We did pay him and got him cigarettes and we had to pick him up and drive him home every day. Plummer's use welding torches to solder pipes together. Our blind plumber was a risky bet to perform his plumber duties. We kept an eye on him while he worked. After two years we sold the ugly house in the bad neighborhood. It was still an ugly house and it was still in a bad neighborhood but it had a bathroom and a new but unattractive kitchen and new paint. My friend and I each made a very little money for our hard work and efforts. But I had just enough money from the sale to get to two times two. Amazing.

I reinvested in myself and got more education and got a little more income. I found a better house in a better neighborhood and the house had a rental apartment that generated an extra income. The banks would not lend me the money for the house just on my income. The house had to be an income earner as well. It was risky to buy a house on my own with not enough income to support it, to be dependent on a tenant who would supposedly pay rent. But I could always get another waiter job to help pay for the house. I was climbing the economic ladder taking more risk along the way. It was scary and it was exciting. The house was undervalued because it needed work and the neighborhood had potential. I had no money for renovations so I took inexpensive courses to learn plumbing, electrical and carpentry. My lab partner in my electrical class was a university professor of sociology. Smart man bad electrician. He often started electrical fires during class. Very risky lab partner. I found my appliances on the street. Appliances that people were throwing out but still worked. I guess they were up grading their appliances.

Upgrading appliances oh to dream of that day. The great stove that I found was the color of mushrooms and the oven door often fell off. It was a treasure to me.

I kept investing in the house and up grading the services and decor and eventually moved out of the house and in with a romantic partner and rented out the two units in my house. This gave me a very good income and along with my day job I was doing very well. Investing in new socks and underwear was no longer a problem. The neighborhood of this house started to increasing in value. I had equity in the house and I was paying down the mortgage. I was ready for four times four. Watch out here I come.

I wanted a second house another income earner and one that would go up in value. I wanted to acquire asset builders and income producers greater than my day job's income. I was afraid to go to the bank. Before I bought my first house with my friend, I tried to buy a house on my own. Ten banks said NO. I was told "you will never own a house your income is not enough and you have no assets." It hurt to be turned down and I was afraid I was stuck forever at one times one. But no one loves a broke coward. I tried several banks for the second house and they all said NO. I reluctantly told a friend my interest in getting a second home. My friend worked in the banking business and he gave me the name of an independent mortgage agent. I made an appointment. When I got to the office, I was told by the secretary I had "five minutes." Five Minutes? Five minutes to say what I wanted and what I had. When the customer before me left the Broker's office I was ushered in and the secretary held up her hand with each figure pointing out reminding me, I had FIVE minutes. As precisely as I could, I explained what I had, and what I wanted. The agent looked at me, took out his calculator, punched in the numbers and said, YES. Four minutes, and it changed my life. I walked the five miles home in the rain. I walked and I walked. And I knew I had a chance. I could break through being part of the 99%. I had a chance and I was going for it. Opportunity was knocking and I was answering the door. I did not see this as a risk, it was more of a risk not to take it.

I had fourteen thousand beautiful dollars for the down payment. I qualified for a $150,000 for a second house. I found a house in a shabby part of downtown within walking distance of the financial district and a major shopping district. At night the women walking back and forth on the street were not anxiously waiting for a bus and the sketchy used car lot, five doors down never seemed to sell a car. The house was twenty feet wide at the front and nine feet at the back. The house was shaped like a piece of pie and it was built in the late 1800. It had wide plank floors, a saggy staircase, ten foot ceilings, fifteen cats and five piss soaked mattresses. I paid $140,000 beautiful dollars for this architectural masterpiece. It had new wiring and plumbing, four bedrooms, two bathrooms and majestic trees in the large back yard. I spent four days cleaning and painting and paid a team of neighborhood homeless guys to help me. I gave away the cats to good homes with ten dollars each for food. I advertised the place to rent and after four days of cleaning and painting I looked out the front window to see a lineup of potential tenants waiting to see the place. I pushed my homeless guys out the back door and prepared to vet the potential tenants. People wanted a down town address and people loved the quirky nature of the house and the original Victorian details. Tenants always paid enough in rent to cover the mortgage and they paid the utilities. I put down $14,000 and sold the place for $800,000 fifteen years later. Best $14,000 investment I ever made. But here's the 1% idea. As the place went up in value I borrowed the equity, called "leveraging "to buy another property that increased in value 1 million. 1% thinking. Bam!

People told me about the risk. Two houses, two beautiful mortgages, what if tenants did not pay the rent. What if you need a new roof, furnace, what if there is a fire and it did not just burn down your house but the neighbor's, on either side of you. What if a tenant or one of their guests' trip, hurt themselves and sued you? What if? Good luck with sleeping at night.

Yes, the money is good. But the thrill of growing creating and striving is pure exhalation. Watching action-adventure movies become ho hum because you are just a passive watcher. Getting in there, making something out of nothing, realizing your dreams, taking yourself out for a run and seeing how far and fast you can go, is a rush that there is no comparison to. The financial rewards are great, but the thrill of the adventure and the knowledge you gain is the big ticket. The bonus is, If I lost it all tomorrow, I know how to recreate what I have accomplished. I have gained the knowledge and the experience of thinking like the 1 %.

Risk Management.

The bramble is what people get stuck in when they are trying to go forward. The bramble is the negative of "what ifs." It is a style of thinking and it can be a way of getting you stuck. The fear of the risk and making a change. I was lucky I came from nothing and I often failed and very little ever came easy. For people who come from many resources, have a great intelligence and easily succeed in school, with a track record of great relationships, they have limited practice with struggle and failure. Some are used to it and expect it. Some believe that struggle is life. Also add in the very good looking. Many in my family are extremely good looking people. Maybe I was adopted. Handsome is not an adjective said in my direction. Doors open so much easier for the beautiful. They are in the fast lane. But they do not like risk, they have had limited exposure to it. Why would they? I am saying if you are of average intelligence, come from limited means and you are not attractive you may have a higher level of tolerance for risk and you should, what do you have to risk, mediocrity? Who knew average has its benefits?

For some people who have had a series of psychological traumatic events in their life they cope by drawing a small circle around themselves. They seek great control over who and what happens in their life. Many no's, many "I can't do that." They are trying to keep themselves safe, but the most opportunities lie outside of your current situation. Fear is a scary thing. It can shut down your life, keep you away from opportunities or it can be a motivator to push you to take chances to find higher ground. Others that have had trauma have learned extraordinary coping skills. They seek help, pull together their resources, encourage themselves to survive.

When people were on the titanic and in the World Trade Towers during 9/11 some chose to stay with what they knew. The ship, the building. The ones that stayed did not survive. The people that sought a way out gave themselves a chance, but it was risky. Of course, some that tried to get off the Titanic did not live and the same with those who tried to get out of the twin towers, but the ones that tried gave themselves the best chance. If you stayed on the Titanic and with the Towers you perished. What is your survival instinct? What chances will you take in life to find higher ground? Go watch an action adventure disaster movie. Will you take the risks that you watch the hero take?

There is a body of knowledge called "Risk Management" that helps people examine financial business deals to help understand the likely hood of success. The bank does this when you apply for a mortgage. The bank calculates your chance of paying your mortgage based on your track record of paying your bills and credit cards. They add up your income, assets and subtract your financial liabilities. They ask the question, "is this person likely to pay what they owe if we lend them the money?"

You can take this idea and expand on it. Take your "What If Questions" and come up with plans to challenge your fears. If a tenant does not pay their rent, what are you going to do? I asked this question to my friend Teddy from Detroit who has several rental properties in his city. "Teddy Spaghetti" from Detroit explained that if someone did not pay rent, he sent his cousin Bubba over to the apartment. Bubba would take the door off the hinges of the apartment and leave it in the hall. Then Bubba would come in, turn on the television, pull down his pants and sit in his underwear on your couch until you paid rent. Bubba ate a lot of food that made him gassy. I explained the legal problems to Teddy for his land lord tenant ideas and Teddy explained to me the culture of Detroit.

If tenants don't pay rent, you need a cash reserve to cover your expenses for a number of months. You need a plan B, C, and D. If you do not have the cash reserve go to plan b, a line of credit, or plan c and low interest cash advance credit card. You can get stuck in the "What Ifs" or you can put resources in place to manage problems. If you get into a legal, tax, termite issue you need professional advice. You are not going to know everything, that is what teenagers are for. Teenagers know everything. Many people are afraid to ask for help not wanting to be vulnerable. If you are going to take a risk you are going to be in unfamiliar situations. You will need to ask for help and accept help. More than the potential extra money you get when you take a risk it is what you learn about yourself and life. The value you get from taking risk is to grow as a person. You will develop new skills and knowledge you did not have before the risk taking. This is the true value. Money can come and go but if you gain the knowledge to create your own economy you can apply this knowledge any place, anywhere. It can be part of who you are and how you see what is around you.

Many people say when they really do not want to take the risk or have the knowledge or experience to start a money-making idea, they say to me "I need a lot of money to start a business." You can use money to start a business. If you want to go in to the car manufacturing business you need millions and millions of dollars to start a car company and you can tell people I want to build cars, it is a life-long dream and I have great ideas for great cars and I would build my cars but I do not have the millions to make my dreams come true. Many people want to buy a house and it costs $100,000. People do not wait till they have this amount, they borrow other people's money. This is a very socially accepted risk in our culture and it is not considered a risk. Borrowing for a business, although it has great potential to earn you an income and a grow an asset, it is considered a big risk. But with risk management ideas in place this risk can be reduced. With big expensive business ideas, you need the skill to raise the money required. Very few people on the planet use their own money to develop a business. They raise the money. They acquire the skill to find who has the money and to make the pitch to get the money.

I think it is better to start a business with no money. This is less risk financially and you learn the true skills of starting a business. Money is a great cover for limited business development skills. Many look at me in horror when I say this because it puts the responsibility on them to take action to make dreams come true. When you work for others, you have less responsibility. The buck stops with you for good or bad when it's your business, ideas, skills, and work ethic on the line. People are afraid that they will look foolish, if their business fails. You put yourself out there when you start a business. It's a risk. You develop resilience if you see yourself through difficult times. You may also gain wisdom and knowledge about business, yourself and life. Or you may not learn any of these things but be left with bitter memories. This is the psychological risk which can be more difficult than financial risk. Developing a business will be challenging. It should be or you are not taking enough risk and you are not trying hard enough.

Your risk management should include managing your psychological risk. It helps to have a mentor, someone you know who has knowledge and wisdom to see you through the tough times of starting a business. Know what relaxes you, takes your mind off your troubles, rejuvenates you when you are beaten down. It helps to choose a project that you are passionate about so that you are pumped up emotionally to take on the problems. Work on being resilient which is a great piece of self-knowledge that gives you the best chances in life.

People do not believe you can start a business with no money but I have seen examples of it. I know a woman who during the 2008 economic melt-down started a clothing store. She had no money for rent or the clothing inventory for the store. What could she do? A number of stores in her neighborhood closed and commercial space sat empty. It was a major recession. She approached several stores and asked to use the space for a month only, no long-term rental agreement. Owners had little to lose, the space was just sitting empty and if the economy turned, they could get a better long-term contract. She found a landlord who would accept the rent thirty days after she occupied the space with a contract that guaranteed the rent payment and a credit card number. She approached several clothing designers who she knew had great product and were looking to unload the samples they created to sell to buyers. Some samples would not be part of the clothing line bought by stores, they would be discarded. My friend offered several designers a 70/30 split. The designer would get 30% of the sale price if the garment sold. The designer would otherwise have given the cloths away or disposed of them. She did not have to pay the designer for the clothes and they had to bring them to her store. The cost was running off the flyers to advertise the pop-up store opening which she hand delivered in the neighborhood. She used her talent to negotiate the deal with the store owner and the designers. The store sold out in three weeks and she started to repeat this formula and gather a customer base in three American cities three times a year. Besides the house she and her family live in, she keeps a home in the South of France. Just saying.

A friend said he had no money to start a business. Nothing. I said good then you have nothing to lose. He travelled to beautiful Cuba and the bed and breakfast place he stayed at had trouble with payment for bookings from international tourists. Cuban's do not have access to the international banking systems like pay pal or a bank account in a foreign country. My clever friend thought he could open a joint bank account with his new Cuban friend and for 10% of booking fees could give his innkeeper a bank account that people could use to pay for their room. The money could be transferred by bank wire to his Cuban friend's Cuban bank account. He talked to his bank about restrictions on the account to protect himself from over indulgence from his new friend. This was his risk management idea to protect his credit rating. This project worked out and several other bed and breakfast inns are getting in on this arrangement.

There is a wealthy area of a city where in the trash treasures are frequently found. Especially at the end of the month when people move there are great finds. A person who hates seeing things wasted and it bothers them how the planet is filling up with garbage could repurpose these things. What if these garbage items were gathered up and sold on line? What if people got word of this planet saving business, or contacted you to get rid of their stuff which could be resold, reused.

If you begin to listen and look you will hear and see where there is an opportunity and a need that you think you could fill. It is good to push the limit on the money issue. Think as creatively as you can to put the deal together without needing to have money. The answer to the no money deal does not always come in a moment it can take time and investigation, research. It is part of the game. Once you are onto it, doors open. Being a curious person helps. "How does that work? What is missing from getting what you want? Who does that?" Curious questions.

There are languages within languages. The language of medicine can be learned such as the nouns that label body parts, bones, tissue, organs. Medical procedures and the verbs that explain them are studied and the adjectives that describe symptoms are learned. People go to medical school to understand this language so they can talk with others in the medical profession.

There is the language of the 1%. Can you guess what it is? Would the nouns be assets, income, freedom and needs? Could the verbs be investing, leveraging, saving? The adjectives passion, curiosity and hard work.

Free Therapy

You can go for therapy and spend a lot of time and money or you can try to make the changes to become part of the 1%. In therapy, good psychological therapy, you get to know yourself and make changes to your behavior and personality that better suit how you treat yourself and how you function in relationships. As you go on your journey to transfer out of the 99% and into functioning in the 1% you are going to run into how you think of yourself and how you relate to other people, for good and for bad. Do you procrastinate and how does that effect your ability to get what you want out of life? How effective are you as a person? Do you get done what you want? How many road blocks do you put in your way when you want to take a course of action? Procrastination, blaming others, giving up too easily, too quickly, limited resilience. Are you good at taking responsibility or is it too often someone else's fault? Do you grow your abilities to handle a new situation? Who holds you back from what you want out of life? If it is a long list you have to look at how realistic this thinking is and are you still functioning as an adolescent and not as an adult. The buck stops with you when you are the 1%.

I learned to play a game when I was starting out to become part of the 1%. When I went to a store or a restaurant, I would play the game "who is the owner?" I began to notice who moved a little quicker, who did the best customer service, who knew where everything was, who seemed happiest and most involved. The buck stopped with them. They took total responsibility for everything. The owner was not in the back of the store complaining about everyone and everything, they were out front and-on-the-move making everything work.

How is your self-esteem? Or what is your relationship to yourself, are you your own best friend or worst enemy? Do you have a peaceful relationship with yourself or are you always on your back, negative and critical? This way of thinking will make it harder to deal with other's negativity and make it harder to have room in your head to deal with day-to-day problems and sleep at night. Tearing yourself down sucks the energy out of a person. Notice how you talk to yourself for positive or negative. I worked with a carpenter who every time he made a mistake had a temper tantrum. He threw tools and called himself stupid and useless. Otherwise, he was a nice guy. His work was almost perfect but it took forever to do anything and there were holes in the walls after his tantrums. Do you have a strong foundation to your personality or are you easily manipulated by others? Do you know how to handle bullies? Do you have good psychological defense mechanisms to keep you safe from difficult people and life circumstances? Do you know how to calm yourself down, relax, recharge or have more dysfunctional coping mechanisms like drinking and drugs? Have you learned to do this psychologically? Do you do simply things to calm yourself like go for a walk, listen to relaxing music to change your mood? Do you control your emotions internally or are your emotions controlled by life circumstances and others? How effective are you? If you want to do something, do you get it done? Can you rely on yourself and can others rely on you? Do people trust you? How are you about your ethics? Do you have standards that you live by or are your standards often forgotten? How do you feel about yourself if you do not follow your standards for being a good person?

Do you constantly compare yourself and your achievements to other people in a negative way and then use this habit to break down your self-esteem? Is yourself care poor? Do you eat properly? Do you have good sleep habits? Do you have rejuvenating activities or activities that leave you feeling tired and listless? Have you developed energizing activities and self-care routines that leave you ready to go forward with your plans and dreams? You will need to confront bad habits when you try to accomplish more in your life.

How optimistic are you? From dreamer to disaster monger, it is an interesting scale. Some are naive with big impractical dreams to the self-dialog "everything is going to go wrong, so why bother, we are all going to die anyway." I have a Russian friend, very hilarious. Things in Russia often do not work, from the elevator to the tap water, expect problems and yet you go on. My friend works as a doctor on the mean streets of St Petersburg. People who have been shot or knifed will complain about pain and about the difficult life in Russia. My friend tells them "What do you expect you live in Russia. Of course, there is pain. Drink more vodka." How much can you function outside of your view of life and see what is real. How much do you take in other's perspective and be open to a different view then yours? A product that you are sure is the answer to every one's problems may be considered an annoying expensive piece of crap by everybody else who sees it. Does your negative point of view have secondary gain of stopping you from taking risk? Does your negativity let you be "right?" If you don't try then of course nothing is going to work out. Very self-fulling. Can you create a sense of hope for yourself psychologically? Do you give yourself things to look forward to such as starting a successful business? Or do you just see the problems, the risks, and bankruptcy, fire and destruction. Can you break down your hopes into tangible goals you can achieve and build toward a bigger goal?

It helps to allow yourself to get to know what is useful about your personality and what holds you back. What gets in the way of what you want? To be honest with yourself and really see what the reality of your circumstances are and be realistic but optimistic about the possibilities. This is what you want to find out. You give ourself a chance to grow if you take on starting a business and you need to be ready for it. It is an adventure.

When you start a business, it is complicated. Your idea for the business may be much criticized. Bottled water, who is going to pay money for what you can get from a tap for free? Dumb idea or a multi-million-dollar idea? New ideas are the most criticized. “If that was a good idea someone would have thought of that before you.” Artists with a new idea of how life is depicted with paint are criticized. Picasso's work was thought to be very strange. He deconstructed the human form. But that was the point. To see yourselves and others in a different way and that opened the possibilities in people’s minds of seeing yourself and the world in a different way. How much criticism can you handle? Do you take criticism and think about it over and over? Does it get into your mind, interfere with your sleep take up so much room in your mind you cannot concentrate and function at the task at hand? Or are you thick skinned? Criticism bounces off you. You stay true to your sensibility and are not too interested in what others think. Maybe learn from the criticism if it is valid or dismiss it if it is meant to only hurt you. Can you change how you handle criticism? Can you learn to compartmentalize, put away in a psychological box the interfering critical thoughts from others? Can you reduce your criticism of yourself, find peace and grace with your flaws? Are you psychologically minded to work through the issues that come up as you change?

How open minded are you to trying new ideas, function in a different way, how will you comfort yourself when you take a

risk outside of your usual way of functioning? When problems happen do you run away or work through? People say they need money to start a business, they really need psychological mindedness to manage the change.
How are you in relationships with others? Are you shy, do not ask for help, never want to bother other people? Developing a business usually requires the best skills in dealing with others. Leadership skills, clear communication, learn to delegate, inspire people, have people work cooperatively for a common goal. Or do you pit people against each other, chose difficult conflict hungry people and give them responsibility and your visa card? Are you a good judge of character with others? How is your anger management? Do people just annoy you or are you inspired by others and like the ideas and tasks you work on together? Are you a team player or does everything have to be your way?

Stubborn is good. It is close to resilience as long as there is room for you to bend to the situation at hand. You need to have staying power if you are going to endure the demands of starting a new business.

I watch as people build businesses around me to learn from their mistakes and their successes. I came from a non-entrepreneurial back ground. My family always worked for others. I had to learn from nothing everything about having a business. It is a different philosophy about working for others and working for yourself. It was tempting to stay with the familiar to not break free of the many ways of thinking that kept me as part of the 99%. There was much criticism about becoming more than what you are.

“Who do you think you are?” “You do not know what you are doing.”

And that was true, but I found out what to do. I took courses and I met people who were doing what I wanted to do. I read biographies of people who developed businesses from nothing. How did they do it? I held myself back, putting roadblocks in my way. I began to keep a journal with just the road blocks. It was easier to do what I could easily do, to continue with what was familiar, but it gave limited results for personal growth. I had to practice the long view. I believed that if I put enough pieces together, I would have a new picture. I did not always know where or if I would find the pieces or if they would fit. I had to work at just keeping going, be hopeful and believe that I was creating something and I was not wasting my time.

I watch people create businesses. Some have business education some do not. The business education seems to have less influence on success. It is more the character of the person. Their work ethic, stick- to- it-ness, and how good is their business idea. Can they put into play their ideas or are they just dreamers? There is luck as part of it but the most important factor is the person. Can they find their way to where they want to go? Intelligence is helpful but lower on the list for success than I thought it would be. The higher the intelligence it seems the less risk a person will take. I think smart people are used to easily succeeding and risk is too unnatural an experience. More average people are used to struggling and more often being wrong. Being wrong is not a threat and it is not a challenging new experience.

What did Walter teach me?

When I was a cog in the wheel, I was also in the company of people who were the 1%. They knew it and I knew it. They functioned in a different way. They made different choices then I did and their choices seemed strange to me, I did not understand why they did what they did. I was taught to fit in, to be a cog in the wheel, to be part of something. Not independent, not a leader. The 1% looked out for their best interests or the best interest of their project with less regard for what is best for the most. They stayed true to their vision, no compromise for other's sake. I thought their behavior was selfish. They were out for their own interests. They knew what they wanted, they had personal priorities and they said no to efforts to push them off track.

But their behavior was respected and considered more valuable. They were paid ten times as much as me. I had a boss who was not part of the 1% but he deferred to the 1% group. He believed that that was the only way to work with them. Anticipate their needs and deliver what they wanted without regard for any self-interest. I did not like this difference in power, or being at the 1% beck and call. But more than anything I wanted to know what they knew. How did it make sense for them to make the choices they made? What did they know that was so different from me? And were they just selfish people out for their own interests or was there something more to understand.

There was one person that stood out as the top of the heap of the 1%. His name was Walter. What did Walter know? Walter followed his own desires. He seemed to do what he wanted with no regard for how it affected others or what was good for the most. He seemed narcissistic from my perspective. But he was not a mean person. He had things he wanted to accomplish, he had responsibilities that he had to meet. Walter had an agenda and no one pushed him off course. He seemed driven more than the rest of us. It seemed like a strange behavior but he guarded his time. He would take his watch off at the beginning of each meeting and place the watch in front of his lovely self on the meeting table and at some prescribed time he got up, grabbed his watch and left the meeting. If you tried to talk to Walter at the elevator and if the elevator arrived, even if you were in the middle of a sentence, Walter got on the elevator. He was on a mission. He taught people around him to not waste his time. To be direct and precise. Just the facts. Walter was generous and he helped many people every day. His specialty was helping the most difficult people that many would not bother with.

Walter was a psychiatrist and helped hard core schizophrenic patients.

Walter's priority was his patients. He was determined to help them. People vying for his time were given limited time. He was the boss of his mission and he was limited to what he could offer others. How he played it out, seemed rude, but he functioned in a different way then I understood. But out of curiosity I would approach a situation as though I was Walter. I asked the question "how would Walter do this?" I would have a goal and work at not letting anything get in my way. I would say no to competing demands to my goal. I set priorities that made sense to me and accomplish them. I would not seek consensus. I did less with the 99%. While my coworkers went to lunch, I raced to the local hardware store to pick up items for the project I was working on. I split time into more meaningful pieces. I limited waste with my efforts. Walter was always on the move and then so was I.

The biggest thing Walter taught me was not to have shame about going after what made sense to me. I was taught to put every body's needs before mine. In many cases this is a kind, civilized approach to life. But some people take total advantage of people who put no boundaries on this philosophy of life. If you develop your own business this is a selfish thing to do. You need to focus on your vision for the business. You need to guard your resources and the businesses resources. Time is an important resource. I had to overcome my guilt for wanting more out of life, more out of life then most of my family, friends and coworkers. "How dare I want to accomplish more. Is not what the 99% of the population have, enough?" Well, no it was not. It was not the money I wanted, I wanted to accomplish more, try my talents out, see if my ideas were sound. See how far and fast I could go.

After working for a while in my government, union protected job I noticed that my staying late, taking on more work, learning to do my job more efficiently was bothering my coworkers. "You are making the rest of us look bad, pace yourself, slow down." But we were hired to work, should you not give your job all of your abilities? This approach was despised by fellow employees. I was considered a poor team player. But what if I took my extra energy and talent and developed a project outside of work where I could be all that I could be. Direct my extra creativity, drive, work ethic and vision for my own project and stop annoying my coworkers. Still do what was required at my job but after hours run with what I might be. I could be Walter outside of work. There was no room for two Walters in the work place anyway.

I knew I crossed a line when I was in a meeting and people who were talking about what they were doing after work that day. We did not often talk about work related issues in meetings. I said I was tearing down a load bearing wall in my house and I was excited about how it would open up the room. My coworkers got quiet.

People stared at me and someone, after an awkward pause said "Who is giving you permission to do that?"

I said "It is my wall I give myself permission."

"But how can you just do that, on your own."

"I use a big crowbar. It will be great."

I realized I had crossed a magic line. I was Walter. I had a plan. I assumed the risk and I took responsibility. I was not waiting for consensus of a group of over seers. I was stepping forward. The 99% were not going to do that. They were staying in a protective bubble of the heard and they would not be venturing out. They felt safe, they thought they were being protected by being part of the most. I was venturing out. They were beginning to see me as the other. The added light to open the room was worth the tearing out of the load bearing wall. The weight of the wall was redistributed to two other walls. I was using my structural engineering knowledge. I managed the risk of moving the wall with what I know about engineering.

I stayed quiet to many about what I was doing outside of work. But when I announced my quitting, many coworkers told me I was making a huge mistake. I did not have enough money to quiet, I would be bored, I did not know what I was doing. I understand the pull of fear of leaving the 99%. Being part of the heard is a powerful draw. But do you realize how much you have to give up to stay the same as everyone else? Your dreams, your vision. It seems risky to leave the heard. But if you think long, and hard it is risky to stay with the heard. Your individuality needs to be stifled. Walter was crude in how he protected his priorities. You can do this with more finesse, grace, and diplomacy.

Breaking free

I found a quirk in my employment contract. If you left the job before you were 55 years old you could take your accumulated pension with you. If you stayed and got your pension you would get a defined amount for the rest of your life. If you continued to read the fine print in the contract it explained that when you got an old age pension from the government that amount would be deducted from the pension you received. When you died your spouse would get half of your pension income. The amount of pension income money seemed low compared to what you could get if the amount was invested on your own. If you took your money out of the pension, that money, when you died could all go to a spouse or child. Also, when you got a government pension it was not deducted from your investment. When talking to the pension representative they strongly advised you to stay with the plan, that was what most people did, it was safest. The amount in the plan was a bit under a million dollars, very good for a civil servant.

I told my coworkers about getting out of the pension before they were fifty-five. Most had been at the job longer and would have had over a million dollars in their pension. This news agitated them. They said I did not know what I was talking about. I gave them the number of the pension office and information about how to find out what was in their pension. They seemed upset and dismissed me, except for one other coworker who wanted to hear more. I was puzzled by my coworker's determination to believe I was wrong, dismissive of the idea that they could possibly have a million dollars. A simple phone call would have given them some important information that would have a huge impact on their economic well-being. But they would not do it. I thought about it a lot. A million dollars, that was yours, that you can control and you could leave to a spouse, your children. You could get a good income from it and actually grow it into a larger asset because you had control over it. What was going on? It was important for me to understand the point of view of my coworkers. They were intelligent people. Why not find out if you really had a million dollars, it would be so easy. I thought about it over time, this was the same group who when they talked about money or investment would say the oddest things. They were a well educated group but they almost bragged about how they knew nothing about investing money and relied on a spouse or a bank manager or financial planner to make all of the decisions for them. They believed it was not possible for them to have the simplest grasp of the knowledge of financial planning. They had university degrees but they could not, would not know about the possibilities of their having a million dollars. It was not how they identified themselves. Their understanding of who they were did not include having a million dollars. That could not possibly be who they were. They could also not be responsible for their economics. A spouse, a financial planner, a bank employee could know this information but they could not. Good middle class civil servants could not possibly have a million dollars. It was as though I was trying tell them that were of a different race or gender, it could not be possible because if it was possible, they would have known. Even more profound, it would change too much in their life. They would have a phenomenal amount of choice regarding their work life and their relationships. They could be free to choose outside of their current circumstances, circumstances that they thought they had no choice about. They were in prisoned in their jobs and relationships and they suddenly could be totally free. A million dollars was the key to their cell. Also, the responsibility lay with them to choose so much more about the circumstances of their lives. They were scared. They did not know how to be outside the herd the 99%. They had never imaged themselves as ever having this possibility.

WOW.

I had to remember that when I first found out this information I had disbelief, as well. I checked seven times with the pension office to see if it was true. I had my doubts. I did note that the pension staff gave direr warnings regarding taking the money out of the plan. I was told stories of hardship and financial disaster, impending economic doom. If many moved their pension money out of the plan they would be out of a job and the new money coming into the plan along with current invested money in the plan paid for the thousands of people receiving a pension. There was an over reliance financially on people staying in the plan and it was a financial threat to the pension to ever have people exit the plan. Stay with the herd. But it was a bad deal. The money was so conservatively invested that it was a very low return on investment and the capital amount which was ours could not be passed on to a spouse or child. If you had a short life after work it was a very poor deal because for a short time your money would only have a limited time to give you a return. The price you pay to belong to the herd is sometimes too much.

Reinventing Yourself

Does a caterpillar know it's future? Does it know in its tiny, tiny brain that one day it can fly? It will not just be assigned the task of slowly crawling from place to place, only able to see the world from the ground or maybe as high as a leaf in a tree. Does the caterpillar dream of the day it can fly and travel thousands of miles to meet the mate of its dreams? Does it know its future, it's possibilities? Does it resist the change that comes to it? The caterpillar will build its cocoon, hoping to be safe long enough to transform into a butterfly with so many more possibilities?

It is a strong pull to remain what you are. It feels safe, it's predictable, it is in human nature to resist change. There are industrial psychologists whose job it is to help people in the work place adopt to change. To help people work through their anxiety, fear and worry about the change in the work environment. The mind set of resistance is very strong and yet there are many examples of people participating in great change in their lives. Some chose change and some it is forced onto them. But people have the ability to adopt and they have the ability to resist change.

People change countries, enter new cultures, learn new languages. Migration is a huge part of many people's lives and the adaptation that goes with it. Years ago, people went to new countries with minimal resources and started over. Many came from Europe with no money, education, social connections and no ability to speak the language. They adopted. They left everything and everybody they knew and took a huge chance and started over with very little means to do it. We live with many safety nets now to protect ourselves financially and socially and yet we seem to live with more fear and resistance to change. I have a friend who came from Europe with no money. When he arrived in his new country's airport, he found a little bag with some coins in it. He remembers thinking how lucky he was and he felt rich. He now owns several houses in a posh neighborhood.

When you live in North America you have a great deal of safety and you are very protected socially and economically. My mother grew up on a farm during the 1930's depression. When she was eight, on her way home from school her job was to gather a herd of cows together and get them to cross a railway line before the afternoon train arrived. In my neighborhood eight year olds are escorted by a responsible care giver with a certified license for child care to get them to and from school. Children are precious and must be cared for but we live in a culture where most risk has been stripped away. It is amazing to see how people new to our culture see so much more opportunity than the people who grew up inside this culture and are so change adverse.

People reinvent themselves all the time. You change skills several times growing up. Change neighborhoods, make new friends, finish school start jobs, move from a parent's home to your own home. People adopt. The sad situation is the person who does not go through the changes of transitioning from school to work, from a parent's home to create their own home. How limited are you to growing and changing? If your work environment changes how adaptable are you or have you developed more change resistant behavior.

You know the language of change resistance. "We have never ever done things that way." "That will never work."

Working in a union protected, civil servant environment comes with great change resistant behavior. It explained why my many coworkers could not imagine a work life outside of what they had done for many years.

To reinvent yourself for some is a natural path. They see the opportunity, see the future as positive, they are excited not afraid of change. Bring it on. Some people become more so as they age. Whatever character traits they have had for good or bad, become more exaggerated as they age. Other's grow in skill, ability, knowledge, they become more. Which path are you on? Which path do you want to be on?

Some abilities will fall away as you age. If you work a construction job your energy and physical strength will become limited as you age. Do you change to a supervisory role and use your knowledge of your trade to guide the young and the strong to perform the job or do you time out with a bad back? Do you burn out psychologically from your professional job or do you plan for a transition to keep your enthusiasm and use your knowledge and experience in a different way that shields you from the every day psychological drain? Do you build an alternate form of income that frees you up from your dependence of you being the employee?

Exercise

Make a list of five things you are going to change. Things you have been meaning to change but procrastinating about. It does not matter how big these changes are. Divorce to new shampoo. The important thing is to make changes so you have the experience of change. The exercise is about finding how you talk to yourself. What is your narrative about making changes? Are you negative or positive? Optimistic or pessimistic. "This new shampoo will make my hair fall out and give me brain damage." Or, "I will be so beautiful I will be adorned by so many and this will help me find a new spouse who will be rich and beautiful." This is an exercise to help you know your attitude about change. How much do you hold yourself back and how much does your attitude contribute to keeping you so very stuck? Do you think you have a negative view and that keeps you safe? Is there a way to go forward and keep yourself safe with some risk management ideas? The negative ideas are yours, own them and decide if you will change them. You may need to learn how to self soothe. How do you talk yourself through a difficult anxiety situation in an encouraging way? "I think I can, I think I can." (from "Thomas the Train.")

Entrepreneur

Along a river set in a gorge there were rocks by the water edge. In the cracks in the rocks, trees had grown. These trees were in the most impossible place. These cracks seemed to have no soil and the gorge was deep enough that no sunlight could find its way to these rocks. And yet here were these random trees, despite impossible circumstances. Somehow a seed had made its way into this crack in the rock and found enough soil and light to grow and even flourish. Being an entrepreneur is like this seed. Entrepreneur's find an opportunity, in impossible circumstances. They seek out the resources to grow even when the resources are difficult if not impossible to find. They thrive in limited circumstances. They have resilience and courage. Did they have these traits before they got started or did, they acquire them as they needed them, to survive? Does it matter? Maybe you have these traits to start and maybe you will get these beautiful traits as you grow. It does not matter.

The term entrepreneur scares some people. If you have always worked for someone else, been part of something, not in charge, then being an entrepreneur can seem very much outside your comfort zone. The term entrepreneur comes with a lot of baggage. Some think that to be an entrepreneur means you must be Eon Musk, and Bill Gates, and Mark Zuckerberg. You must be at the helm of a billion dollar business on the leading edge of technology and you must be a nasty, hard driving, take no prisoners person. Calm down. Most entrepreneurs are people with a plan to support themselves, start and run a business. If you have never worked for yourself, been in charge, have the buck stop with you, you may be scared by how unfamiliar you are with this way of functioning. There is a lot to be learned by understanding the behavior and personality of the entrepreneur. (If the term entrepreneur bothers you use the word kitten instead.)

Entrepreneurs (kittens) are in business for themselves. They have an idea for a business and they want to develop it. They are in charge of the business; the buck does stop with them. They carry the responsibility themselves. This seems like a road block for many, the responsibility. The creation, the day-to-day operation responsibility for a business seems over whelming to many and so they are very hesitant to go forward. Part of the fear is fear of the business failing and more so, the criticism from others. "You do not know what you are doing!" Well of course not. Knowing what you are doing is over rated. Thinking on your feet, rising to the challenge, that is the better way to go. You learn to be open to learning. The most critical people are the ones who have never tried to start a business because of their own fear of responsibility and criticism. Many who have started a business know that it is difficult because there is a great learning process, great risk and hard work. It is also a more exclusive club because more people would rather stay working for others avoiding the responsibilities and risk. But they stay with the 99%. Most entrepreneurs have the experience of having their business ideas not work out. What true hardcore entrepreneurs have is resilience and what they are doing is learning from their mistakes and moving toward the ideas that work. They fall down and they get up with increased knowledge and ability to make it work next time. Their belief in their ideas is so strong they do not have a lot of psychological room for other's criticism.

Entrepreneurs have a process to be learned from. They have a business plan. They have a goal with time lines, and a narrative regarding how they are going to get their goal accomplished. Often these plans are written with the idea that a bank or money person is going to read it to fund the business plan.

It is interesting to think of yourself as someone who is in business for yourself. You are so and so INC. What is the nature of your business? Who is your target market? What is your process to create your product? What is the marketing strategy? Think of yourself as the boss. It is your company what are you going to do? It means taking on the role of a leader with an increase in responsibility. Begin to delegate, make the risky choices. Develop the business, make it grow. Some people are surprised to find their inner boss. Sometimes the quietest, mousiest person are really a want-a-be boss, general, commander. The things you may find out about yourself on your way might surprise you and shock others.

"I always thought she was so quiet. She did not know what she wanted and she let others boss her around. Well look at her now."

Can you become entrepreneurial? Well let's find out. You could read biographies of entrepreneurs and learn their personality traits, choices they make and what they did to become entrepreneurial. You could look for these traits in yourself. Think of people in your family who are entrepreneurial. What makes them who they are? Is it their personality traits, the choices they make, their behaviors? How are you like them? Take them out for lunch and ask them questions about how they grew a business, came up with their ideas, what motivates them. Be open to learning.

Become an entrepreneur for the day. What will you do as an entrepreneur? What will you have for breakfast? Put together an entrepreneurial costume. What will you wear? What will be on your schedule for the day? Business meetings at a bank, take a meeting with people to brain storm business ideas, a power lunch at a place where business people gather. Sit in on a rezoning application at city hall to watch land developers pitch a proposal. Will you just observe, or will you cross over and start putting into place real activities where you are growing an idea. These ideas have very little cost. Ask the question "If I was an entrepreneur what would I be doing? Cross the line and get started. Waiting is over rated.

Exercise

Look up on line "business plans." Pick one that works for you. Create a brief outline of what your business is about and write an
operation plan for the business. How will you create your business?
What is the practical stuff you need to do to make it work?
Write your goals and time lines for the business.
Where will you find the money for the company and how inside the company will the money generate a product or service. How will the money come out of the business and back to you?
How will you keep up your spirits during difficult times? Who will be your mentor?
What personal qualities keep you resilient, stubborn, optimistic? How are you, your own best friend in good and bad times?
Write yourself a letter before you start. Like a letter to a friend to encourage them when they are lost, discouraged, unsure.
Make a 911 list. What to do when you are lost and unsure.
Words of encouragement, and good advice.

"If you can get a person who is a communist interested in your business plan you have a good business plan." L G

Money

I was at the bank the other day and the helpful bank employee congratulated me on having a tidy sum in my account and said she hoped one day to be a good investor but explained that she believed you have to have money to make money. I explained that I came from nothing and believed you do not need money to make money. She shrugged in a gesture of disbelief.

I have heard it said "It is easy to say you don't need money to make money when you have a lot of money."

It is also possible to disbelieve my statement when you do not have the knowledge or the willingness to take the risk to start a business. You want to believe that you have to have something you don't have so you don't have to work through your anxiety of the risk of becoming something that is so different from what you are.

I asked the bank person how much she had to invest. She, with a sad voice said she had a $1,000. I said that was a $1000 too much to start a good investment. She turned away wanting to dismiss my crazy statement but something got her to ask "So how would you get started?" It was a provocative dare.

I explained "I think you are too distracted by your thousand dollars. You think it is not enough to do anything. You are overly focused on what you don't have. The focus needs to be on what the investment could be. Whatever you invest in needs to have potential to grow. Find the growth, the resource in the investment. If you bring money to the investment, it can influence the timing of starting the investment, but you can use time in a different way to manage money with a business."

When wall to wall carpet was popular a man would sell housing developers the carpet, they needed to finish their homes. He got orders from the developer for the amount of carpet they needed at a particular price and he approached the carpet manufactures and bargained down a wholesale price for the carpet needed at 20% cheaper than the developer was going to pay. He had no manufacturing costs, no warehouse, show room or sales staff. No overhead investment costs. He was the middleman at 20%. He did not buy the carpet, display the carpet, he just connected the manufacturer to the buyer. He had limited overhead. He did not need a thousand dollars. He had a phone.

The bank lady was aware that I had bought properties and explained how expensive property was in the city and how she wanted to invest in property but a thousand dollars was not enough of a down payment.

Again, I recommended she not focus on the thousand dollars, it was too distracting. I explained that the last property I bought had so much value in it, that the bank was not very interested in my assets and income but was more interested in the assets and income of the property. The tenants of the property paid more money in rent then the mortgage payment would be. The tenant paid all utility bills and property taxes. The rent after the mortgage payment gave me an income of $600 a month. This is called positive cash flow. But the property was significantly undervalued per square foot than any other property in the neighborhood. The building, with some minor cosmic changes, would be more valuable than its asking price. (This is a nice way to say it was an ugly building.") If a significant addition was added to the place, it would be significantly more valuable. The difference in the actual value of the building compared to the price of the building was enough equity to borrow on to pay for the addition to the building. The neighborhood was radically changing for the better and that would increase the value of the building even if nothing was done to it. It was not what I brought to the investment it is the value that was in the investment itself.

Michael Angelo taught this concept with his work called the 'slaves.' He had large pieces of marble and he partially completed a figure in the stone. He left the work undone to demonstrate that within the rock was a form that was unique to the large piece of marble. Look within the marble for what form existed. Do not impose a figure onto the rock, the structure of the rock may not tolerate the form, but peel back the meat of the rock to find what is possible within the rock. Find the value within the investment. Keep looking for the investment that has great potential for an increase in value as an asset and for income. That needs to be the focus, not the dollars you bring to the investment. If you find the value in the project and can show it to others the money will come. You need to look deeper into the investment to find the value and not focus on what money you bring to the project. Look for investments in a down market that is best. There is less money available in difficult economic times so you will make the leanest choices and often find some great deals. An abundance of money brought to a business deal will let you be sloppy regarding finding the most opportunities inside the deal. There is a saying "buy low sell high." Profound. So, few act on this concept.

One day Mary was riding home on the bus from work and she looked out the bus window at the guy next to the bus driving a BMW and wondered "why am I not in that nice car?" She knew she was smart and worked hard so what was the difference between that guy and her? Money or how to make money? Mary had time to think about this on the slow, stop and go ride home on the hot sinky bus. She thought she had no assets to invest to grow an asset and no time or energy to work another part time job. She felt stuck. Mary, that evening started to clean her lovely apartment. She often cleaned when she had something to think about. Mary wanted to figure out how she could go forward economically when she had no extra money from her work. She put most of her income into her great apartment, with the beautiful view, in a great part of the city. Her apartment meant a lot to her and it was larger than she needed because she was on her own. She was happy with how she had decorated the place, well-chosen furniture and paint colors. Friends often admired her place. Mary cleaned and cleaned that night wondering what she could possibly find as a way to go forward economically to improve her situation.

Find the money in the product or in the deal, that is your focus not how much money you have. Even if you have money do not get distracted or sloppy by this detail, look within the deal for the economic potential. The untapped asset and income. And look for both the asset and income, not just one or the other. Go for both. Why would you not? Both are important but many make the mistake of just looking for either one, not both. If you want to get to 16 times 16 you need to grow assets and income. This is what is required for exponential growth and is a corner stone in thinking like the 1%.

Some with too much money make investment mistakes in the other direction. Yes, you are crying for them. Have tissues at hand. I hear people with large investment amounts believe they can only do deals with a great deal of money. One acquaintance had three million to invest and would limit what he would consider as an invest only if the investment required that amount. Rather snobby, very limiting. My friend's priority was the 3 large to invest, he did not focus on the value in the deal. His return for his investment was very low maybe $100,000 return over a number of years. This is a very limited return for this amount. But more important he did limited risk, limited learning or personal growth with this way of investing. He made his $100,000 but that is all he got, he never developed his knowledge of risk, he never learned to find the value in the deal, he did not grow his knowledge or abilities as a person. He missed the real opportunity.

Taxes not death

I was running with a friend of mine who is truly a genius. Poor man has to deliberately dumb down what he says because he thinks like a scientist's scientist. One day we were also running with a third friend who was a tax account. My scientist friend was bragging that he was using his real estate invest as a tax loss against his super magnificent high income. I explained this was stupid. My scientist friend had never, in his whole life, have anyone said that word directly to him. He explained that because his tenant was paying him less money than the cost of the monthly expenses of the condo, he could write this loss off against his giant big super income. I explained that "more is more." If he made more money from the rental of the condo then the expenses of the condo and God forbid pay more tax, he would be making more money. He could not, would not believe me. He turned to our account friend for confirmation of his breath-taking knowledge on this matter. Our accountant friend said I was correct. Our science friend is a most excellent scientist, very gifted in his knowledge of science.

It is not what you make it is what you keep. And damn it, pay your taxes. We need roads, hospitals and schools for the children. But you also need the knowledge of how the tax system works so you will make the best business decisions and a record of the tax you pay is most helpful to get loans from banks. If you pay a lot of tax that is good because it means you made a lot of money. If you made a lot of money, it means you must have ability, skill, talent, work ethic or something that allows to earn a lot of money. It means you are honest and are likely to pay back what you borrow and you have the income to pay back what you owe.

But you will make better business decisions if you understand taxes. The tax system is designed to encourage the 1%, to reward them and with the thinking the 1% will create jobs and grow the economy for the many. This is sort of true. But the biggest deal is the tax system lets the 1% pay a significantly smaller portion of their money in tax. When I had crawled my way into the shallow end of the 1% and needed to pay tax accordingly, I thought I was grossly misunderstanding the tax obligation. It just could not be. Basically, if you make a big pile of money quickly it is capital gain and you pay a much smaller percentage of tax. If you are a regular wage earner, getting the same income week after week this is called income and it is taxed at a huge percentage more than capital gain.

Look it up yourself. Every country and in every area of a country has a tax system that is a little bit different and it is an ever-changing set of rules. But the basic rule applies. Make big money fast and pay a much smaller percentage in tax and a regular smaller week to week income gets a bigger percentage of tax. This is why “the rich get richer and the poor get poorer.” You need to understand this. This is why you should not rely just on your lame income; you need to grow an asset; it is subject to a lower tax rate. Get in on this and hurry up.

Also, when you are growing an asset, you are given “tax breaks.” The money you use to fund the growing of your asset is tax deductible. What you invest in your company or asset building is subtracted from the gain in the value of your asset. For your day job there is hardly any money you can deduct from your taxable income. The car you use to get you to your boring job is your expense, no deduction from your taxable income. The car you use to go to business meetings where you discuss growing your business is usually tax deductible. In some places your $100,000 car is a deductible expense while your eight-year-old ford used to commute to work is not considered a tax deduction. Think about it, but more important check it out. Know your tax system so you will make the best business choices. This knowledge is available from your tax department. It is easy to find this information and not that difficult to understand. Just hard to believe if you are in the 99%.

What you need to search for is what is the definition of what income is and what capital gain is and tax charts on income and tax rates on income and capital gain. Be prepared for shock and ah. What, you who makes so little pays higher percentage of tax? Yup. And you need to be aware of the extra ways to shield your money from tax. Yes, there are more write offs for the high-income earners but your money can be organized in ways to delay paying tax so you can use the money to continue to build an asset. Having a numbered company holds your assets in a way that it protects your money, and your assets until you cash out. The 99% have some lame asset protectors so you can protect your accumulated money until you are old and cannot work anymore, have no income and you are close to death. 41ks or rrsp. There are many restrictions on these asset protectors for the 99% that do not leave you eligible for many investment possibilities. But the 1% have numbered companies that shields their asset money. They have trust funds for their children, they have tax deductions that shield money used to grow an asset builder. You have got to get in on this. This is where the opportunity is in this beautiful capitalistic culture, that you were born into. This is why this is the land of opportunity. Go and get you some of this opportunity.

Don't just get a brain freeze and tune out thinking taxes, that is for accountants. No NO NO. This is a vital part of your culture's DNA that helps people grow their economy. Figure it out. You learned something to be able to do your job now learn what can make you rise above. Truly it is not that hard. You don't need to know the tiny details of your beautiful tax system. You just want to know the basic under lying ideas. How is income taxed, how is capital gain taxed? Or how much is your income taxed and how much are you taxed if you make a big heap of money all at once (capital gain)? Find out about deductions. There are tax advantages that are very limited risk where you delay paying tax so you can use your money to invest and grow. Do it, find out.

Fear of change, change the fear.

Many people are afraid of spiders. All those legs. Could crawl into your mouth, when you are asleep. Lay eggs in your ear. Infect your brain. You are 1000 times bigger than the spider and you have two feet that you could use to snuff out the spider's tender life.

If you stand at the front of the plane upon take off, you will see people falling off to sleep, looking for a movie to watch, reading a book. But there are the few who have a death grip on the arm rests, hanging on for dear life, looking out the window checking for engine malfunction, smoke. Same experience, different reaction.

I am fascinated about who crosses the line from the 99% to the 1%. It is not the smartest people or the people with business education or the most handsome, thank goodness for me. I had a friend for years who did what I did as a day job but for half the wages. He was better at the job than me, had more education, and he was smarter than me. I he-ranged him to get a job for more money. We also talked about investing money. He was fascinated about what I was doing but he always shook his head and said "not for me." It just seemed too risky or too something. But it is was more than comfort with risk. The investing for a possible big capital gain and income was not how he could think of himself. To put himself in a place to be a well-off man seemed like an unnatural fit. How a person defines themselves is a more important place for them to be than working to change, to be different even if there are great opportunities within their abilities to achieve. People hang onto what they think of themselves very tightly. There is no tolerance to being different for how they think of themselves it takes a lot for some people to do anything to redefine themselves outside of their economic or social place.

My friend eventually bought a condo as an investment. He paid $300,000 and the condo's rent barely was enough to cover expenses, but this was his comfort zone. He was very cautious with his leap into this level of investment and he had many fears and many worries. Being the good friend that I am I bugged him about buying a second condo in the same building. Well why not? He looked terrified when I would say these ideas. He needed time to regroup and think about himself and life in a new way. He eventually got a much better job than me. Lots more money, the summers off, big pension. He eventually bought the second condo in the building. Each condo is now worth more than a million, each. I try hard to be a good friend.

Another friend would complain to me about his job. Too much bureaucracy, negative work environment. He worked as a nuero scientist. He had a doctorate in science and he did world class research. He worked long hours and his pay was limited according to his seniority, not his work achievements. There were unrealistic expectations, and no promotions. I had talked to him about looking for a better work environment and some ideas about creating a way to grow an income and assets outside of his work environment. One day he told me he quit his job. He was afraid but also excited. He was going into the cell phone business. I was shocked. He had devoted his life to research science, he had incredible science education. I asked if he could get his job back. I could not picture him in sales and cell phones. In two years, he makes ten times what he made before, but more important he feels free. It was not an easy transition, especially for me. I worried about his leaving a career he had been so dedicated to. He had to think customer service, build relationships with people, engage with people in a very different way. He likes to learn and he used this ability to get to a new way of functioning. He is very energized these days and sees never ending expanding possibilities with what he is doing. He hit a wall in his work place and saw nowhere to go. He felt lost and trapped and took a leap to something completely different. He took the risk and it worked out. He is happy and I am relieved.

A third friend has degrees in business. He has worked in business and sales. He has done import, export and product development. He has had 250 employees working for him. He is a very intelligent man, a great problem solver, and hard worker. He has been given many ideas to start his own business. People around him see his potential. He has been given seed money to start his own business. He explained to me that he can only see himself working for others. He does not want to go out on his own. He believes that he needs someone to give him direction and whatever the job or business he is in, he could improve that business. The improvement of someone else's business, he believes is his skill, his strength and that is how he sees himself. But I am not done with him yet.

Exercise

Find a product that you are curious about, that you have an interest in.
Find an undervalued product that has income potential and could grow in value.
Hopefully it is the same product.
Yes this is work, unless it is something you have a strong interest in, then it is not work it is play time.

Out liar

You could think what you want is the money of the 1%. Well, who wouldn't? But more important is the way of thinking, the philosophy. You want to have the knowledge to make the better choices that continually puts you in a place to own your own economy to have economic freedom. You need to make a shift from the ties that bind you to the 99%. It is very seductive to be part of a herd. It feels safer. It is basic primal mentality to want to be within the larger organism of the many. Living as an out liar seems more dangerous, more vulnerable, more worry some. It seems sensible to follow what most chose. Avoid judgement, criticism seek acceptance. Being more out on your own requires more responsibility for the choices you make. Everybody else is doing it that way, who am I to question? Being part of the 1% seems more dangerous. More self-reliance is required. Are you up for the challenge of being out on your own? Can you handle the questioning of your judgement, the pull by many to go back into the safety of the herd? Can you handle your own self dialogue that pulls you back to the familiar, the usual?

But consider what you have to give up to be part of the herd. You have to give up your individuality. Your unique way of seeing things and doing things. You need to suppress to fit in. You must do, think, have, what the crowd has. Aspirations outside of the herd is discouraged. The 1% are admired and despised and you can think it is just the money they have, but it is more than that. It is more the greater freedom they have, to have a broader range of choices with money but even more valuable is greater freedom. You live your life in a more unique way that makes the most sense to you. You march more to your own drummer. It is not a perfect utopia to be part of the 1%. There is a whole industry developed to judge the 1% to critique what they do, wear, judgement about their relationships and how they live their life. People will love and hate you as part of the 1%.

Do you have what it takes to resist the gravitational pull of the 99%. First of all, do you truly have the desire to exist more on your own? Is your freedom more worthwhile than being part of the herd? Is your individuality more precious than your sense of fitting in? Can the need to belong be fulfilled in a different configuration than what you have now. How capable are you to go through a process to reinvent yourself? Are you capable intellectually of being more independent? What is your self-reliance score or should you stay in the 99%? Is it truly safer for you and a better fit for your abilities and level of responsibilities? I know several intelligent, hardworking people who are better to follow the crowd because their judgement around money, business and practical choices are repeatedly poor. They are good workers, and followers, not good leaders for their own life. What is your track record around independence? Have you really allowed yourself to venture outside the herd to find out what you are capable of? Are you capable of existing more on your own but have never tried?

If you are going to venture outside of the herd you must learn to protect yourself, you cannot rely on the protection of the herd. Your unique ideas need to be protected. There are sharks waiting outside the herd to take from you your best ideas, your best efforts. Some of your best personality traits that make you a good part of the herd, make you most vulnerable on your own. There is a shift in sensibility to be out for your best interest, rather than go with the flow be part of something. In business there is usually a contract. Read it. Do not just be complimented that you are in a situation where there is a contract, someone wants something you have. Does the contract become part of the protection of your idea, work efforts? It is your job to protect, prioritize what you are creating. Many people have a parental instinct and apply that sensibility that keeps your children safe and watching out for their best interest. You must apply this sensibility to what you are creating. You must look out for your business's best interests. You must protect it as you bring it to life.

Exercise

Make two beautiful lists this week. On one list put the issues you will do for other's benefit.
The second list is for yourself. A completely selfish list. Accomplishing the items on the list need to only benefit you, for your personal gain. Note your "self-talk" and feelings as you work through each list. Guilt, fear, resentment. Do your feelings dictate your behavior? Can you have a more rational discussion about these feelings? Can you challenge these feelings and behave in a different way?

Part of protecting yourself is guarding the time you need to create it. The power of NO to ward off poor use of your time. You have a priority now and it is time to make it an important priority. You may have practiced many years of being available to others as they needed you. The pull of the herd. Serve the need of the herd. You need to switch your sensibility to make your business development your priority. Boundaries need to be applied to your time and resources. Being passive, quiet and fitting in, needs to change. Take initiative and go for what you want.

It is good to ask for people's opinions to learn what others know, this is different than seeking approval. You need to go through the process of disconnecting from the herd of the 99%. You may feel guilt for wanting to have more out of life. There is some religious ideology that the meek will inherit the earth and rich people cannot get into heaven. But in the Christian religion there are stories of sons who are given opportunity and are scorned for not developing it. No matter what your religious thinking you may have to contend with some personal religious ideas that are a road block to going forward. Some realize that if they do well financially, they are in a great position to help those less fortunate.

Feeling like you are leaving people behind can become a road block. As you grow an idea and a business you will have less time for people in your life. Hopefully you will get to a place where the business supports you and you have more time to be with the people you care about. People around you as they watch you put your time and concentration into a project may be resentful that your attention has left them. Sometimes you can include them or you aim for quality time not quantity time.

Most profound is the changes you make to your personality. When you grow a business, you will change. You will become more self-reliant, more assertive, more confident and more stressed. As you develop more skills in your personality to be more effective you are likely to be more assertive with people in your personal life. The weaker more passive ways of behaving are likely to be replaced with more direct, assertive communication. You will set more boundaries to protect your time and what you are creating. People will note that you have a new loyalty and may question it if that competes with your loyalty to them. You will have higher expectations of yourself and maybe others. You are going to change. Many relationships can change and are stronger for these changes. But some relationships work only if you remain subservient. As you become successful and more independent financially and have more skills you are not as dependent on others financially or psychologically for their approval. You are less likely to be manipulated by others. Some people around you will respect the changes you make and some will think you have abandoned them and have moved on. Some will be jealous of what you have accomplished because they did not grow. Often these issues can be worked through in a relationship.

We are told many things about who we are from parents, teachers and siblings as we grow up. Some of these messages are true, some are inaccurate. Some we outgrow and some messages are manipulative to get us to behave in a passive way. As you grow a business you are probably going to run into challenges to these ideas about yourself. For example, one fellow was told repeatedly that he was lazy. And being an obedient child, not wanting to challenge a parent's sensibility, behaved accordingly. This fellow made choices through the self-perception that he was a lazy person. "I would try that but I am lazy and I won't see it through." But he had a burning idea for a business he wanted to create for electric transportation, bikes, scooter, motor cycles. He got a commercial retail space and with his strong interest in all things electric filled his store with interesting devices of electric transport. He also thought he was saving the planet and this appealed to his altruistic values. He put many hours into finding the best products and his enthusiasm for his products was a draw to his customers. His work ethic toward this business went against his ingrained idea that he is a lazy person and he began to question why he ever had this idea about himself and how often he had made poor choices in his life due to this faulty way of defining himself.

A friend wanted to start a business. She is very bright, great with people and needs to grow financially. But she lists off the many reasons why she cannot start a business. The biggest reason is how she usually gets things for herself. She has a highly developed way of being helpless and appealing to others sympathy to be provided for. She explained to me.

“Look at me I am a little person and people have always felt sad for me and want to help me.”

She has not practiced using her intelligence and hard work to grow an independent business. If she grew a business she would have to work through her dependency and lack of responsibility for herself.

Another fellow did not do well in math classes and had become phobic regarding all things to do with math. He avoided situations where math was involved. Opportunities for jobs that had anything that involved numbers were avoided. Very limiting. He had a great idea for a business he wanted to start, but business involves money, taking it in, counting it etc. But he was burning up thinking about his business idea to sell a particular juice product that he thought was so healthy and tasty. He also thought of all the people he could employ in an area of the country where there was limited employment. Despite his number phobia he went forward with the business. He went slow. He started with talking with the bank about getting a loan and interest rates and amounts for payments. He got spread sheets and wrote out numbers with the help of an accountant friend who talked him through the numbers. He felt his anxiety each step of the way but he stayed with it and slowly confronted and worked through his fears. He had a phobia about numbers, but that did not mean he could not do math or work with numbers. It opened many opportunities for him as he took the toxic air out of this dark part of his ability to function. Starting a business brings forward any deficits you have in yourself or in dealing with others. The ways that you have of defining yourself you get a chance to face and a chance to work through. If you have a business that you are passionate about you will have a powerful motivator to work through these issues. On the other side of developing a business you will have grown emotionally. You will be a stronger person with more skills and fewer road blocks that get in your way of where you want to go. Staying part of the 99% stops you from going through this chance to grow personally. This is psychological growth. The money is great if it comes, but it is the psychological growth that is the most valuable. More confidence, more skills as a leader, and a chance to overcome faulty negative perceptions of yourself are side benefits of growing a business.

Create Creativity

Create a space in your life for your creativity to grow. Creativity needs time and nurturing, not road blocks and criticism. Having a child put me on a quest to know the better parenting skills. The better parenting was giving kids a place to create, to exercise their imagination, and yes this means making a mess. So, buy a large plastic tarp and let them have at it. You get to know yourself through what you create. Much parenting is no no no rather than “can I help you with that, what do you need?” The 99% are not reaching for the stars or the moon. But progressive parents put pressure on kids to do well in science and math, that’s where people think the money is. But that is not where the 1% money is, it’s in the new idea in science and math and for that you need creativity. Steve Jobs, Elon Musk, Edison they used science and math but they added creativity and invented new revolutionary ideas. That's the big ticket. Your creativity is an incredible expression of yourself. What you create is very personal and what people are most proud of. The 99% focus on blending in, not standing out, not going for the unique, the new idea, they seek the similar, the familiar, the same. Child rearing for the 99% involves the blending in, "nobody else is wearing a purple and lime green sweater. With a sweater like that you will not lose your kid in the crowd at the mall. Do not to be afraid for yourself or your kid's out liar ideas.

If you get your creativity on and your ideas are good, you will need to learn to guard what you have created. The 99% don't need to protect very much because so many have what they have. If you have good ideas, you will know it because people will want to steal your ideas, and make your ideas their own. They will want your time, talent and the extra money you make. Inside the 99% you don't need to learn to protect anything you don't have much that any one wants.

The spark, the idea

To become the 1%, you could do it for the money and the economic freedom, but I suggest you ratchet it up a notch. It is hard to break free from the crowd. The pull to conform is daunting. To break from your usual takes a lot of energy and it may not work out. I suggest you develop a business because you want to. Because you have to, because you have no choice. You have something you want to do that it is so important to do that you cannot think of a reason not to do it. You want to provide the world with the best damn perogies anyone has ever tasted. You want to save the planet by providing the best reusable water bottle ever invented. The art you create has to be seen by as many people you can image. You have an idea that you want to express and share with others. You need to find an idea that you burn up with passion for. You will conquer all, lift the heaviest load, cross the most treacherous pass to get your idea out where it belongs. And it would be great if the money came along, but it is part of your personal development to grow, as you grow a business, that is the real value.

The 99% do not have many sparks of passion. It helps to stay in the herd. Passion is very personal, not a great trait to help you fit in. If you are part of a singing choir your great ability to sing out will not be appreciated. They will want you to be part of the choir not fighting to be the soloists. Part of what you need to do is find out if you have been suppressing your passion, your voice. Do you discourage yourself from saying what you really want to say and do? Do you do the "right thing" to be a good boy or girl. You really want the chocolate cake and you want it first, not the lean stake and potatoes. You only put others before yourself. You do not know what you want. It is easier to seek out what others think and want and go with that. Kind yes, thoughtful yes, approval seeking, yes. Very 99%. You have an idea that you have a strong interest in and you talk yourself out of walking forward with it.

"That will never work, nobody will buy my porgies, I do not know how to run a business, I do not have the money."

You can learn and you do not know until you try. Do you know how to talk back to your negative and discouraging thoughts? Most people know how to talk to a child who is afraid and worried about trying something new, because so many things are new. Starting school, making a friend, dating. People know how to say encouraging words to help a child go forward, overcome their fears and accomplish what they want. Can you encourage yourself? Or put yourself in the company of encouraging people, or hire a therapist to teach you to be supportive to yourself.

Develop your process to find your passion and your best ideas. Find a place to go, a thing to do that inspires you. Get up early and find a place to watch a sun rise. Find a body of water, a stream, lake, ocean and sit by this body of water, relax and create a space for your best ideas to come forward without judgement. Go to a place with a breath-taking view, bring a picnic of your favorite food and let yourself image your best ideas. Create a space where you close out the distraction of your usual and create. Let your mind wonder, daydream find your way to new creative ideas. Break your routine in a meaningful way to allow for your best thoughts to develop.

When I do business meetings and I want creativity, big bold ideas, inspiration, I take the group to a place they have not been before, put them in a situation that has an 'ah' inspiring view/experience and set them free to think and create. It energizes the group and it energizes me to be part of a creative experience. Yes, it is good for business but it is the most important part of the whole experience. Building, creating, developing something, something that is amazing, and something that helps others is a great joy.

A friend who builds weird quirky houses, who says a house is a sculpture. He is very creative, very artsy and talks about the "creative process." He puts himself inside creative spaces, art galleries, haunted old mansions, volumes warehouses and thinks. Different architectural spaces for different architectural creative thoughts. Spaces to help spark the minimalistic sensibility. A Moorish, monastic simple space of a cloister, a nunnery to create a minimalistic modern sensibility to a new space. How does the light enter the space, what materials are used, what is the competition of the forms and shapes? He "inhabits" the space till he absorbs the architectural sensibility and applies it to his work. The creative process is amazing, inspiring, gagster, rock star awesome. Find yours.

I am aware of a small food business. A "picos" business. It is a shack in the corner of a parking lot and it makes and sells, ham and cheese sandwiches only. There is a line up all day, every day in front of this shack. A friend interested in this business took a note pad, a picnic and a couple of bottles of water and sat and watched the workings of this business all day. He took notes. Who were the customers? How long did they wait for their sandwich? How did the staff act toward the customers? What made this snack shack work? The product, the staff, the location? My friend's 'curiosity' helped develop his idea, helped take his idea deeper, made it more profound. This exercise helped him be thoughtful about the possibilities. The added information about what he saw gave him many new ideas for his own business.

Everyone thinks they are a great cook, lover, driver. The reality is different. Everyone thinks they are open minded. I cannot stop laughing at the contradiction to this. People to stay intact psychologically have many perimeters to how they think about themselves, life, other people. They usually hold onto these beliefs more than be open to the reality. But this leaves you limited to the many possibilities of life. Every great city in the world has the potential to teach you something if you are open, if you put aside your sensibility of the culture you come from. In Paris you can learn that beauty is important. The clothes you wear, the food you eat, the place you live. The esthetic is important. To surround yourself with beauty is critical to having a beautiful thoughtful life. New York teaches you that striving to be the best is important. The best of the best come to New York to compete at the highest level every day. And NOW is not fast enough in New York.

"What do you mean NOW, I wanted this done yesterday. Now is too late."

In Havana Cuba you can learn that beauty and business is not important because the best in life are the people in your life. The people that you love and love you back. In Cuba there has been no consumer culture for years and no work is more important than the beautiful people in your life and the laughter and joy you have together. But are you open to seeing these lessons from these great cities or have you settled for staying where you are in your routine and not exposing yourself to other ideas, ideas on this planet? Or do you deliberately explore with curiosity the best ideas of this life? Can you take in new ideas presented to you or are you ridged and hang onto what is familiar even when the philosophies of your culture hold you back? Do you live in a small space with limited ideas and possibilities?

In the North American culture, we live in a very protected bubble, economically and politically. Many people on this planet do not have this level of protection. The price we pay for this is to conform. Other cultures do not have these elaborate safety nets socially and economically. Most people must be more responsible for themself especially economically. We can often afford to live on our own but this means we do not really have to learn the more complex social skills to exist with others. We do not have to value our relationships with others because with our littlest of jobs we can get our own housing and not have to be with others. The worst is for elderly people who with their life savings, can afford to live on their own, the most vulnerable time of their life and the loneliest.

Being open minded is critical to expanding your horizons when breaking free of the culture of the 99%. How does the 1% think? It is going to be different, unfamiliar. Can you put down your defense mechanisms allow new ideas in regarding how to live your life. When you go to Paris will you surround yourself with what you are familiar with, and if so why bother to go to a different place. If you have to eat at McDonnell's in Paris and find yourself complaining that it is not the same as what McDonnell's is, at home, you took the plane but you did not get there. You are in the bubble. It seems safe because it is familiar. But familiar is not always safe it's just familiar. How available are you to new ideas, or are you too closed and it is too important for you to stay that way? To become part of the 1% is about reinventing yourself. This is a process. It is about adopting new behaviors, attitudes and new ideas. To practice this, travel to a new place. If your response is. I cannot afford to go to Paris, then travel to a different part of your city or town that you are unfamiliar with, try out different food, watch other people's behavior. Open yourself to a new experience and be open to learning. Some can crack the shell of their existence and some cannot. Who are you? Where is your bravado about the life you are going to live? Where is your bravery to live outside of the familiar? Are you enough for yourself?

Spend time with some elderly people. Some elderly are full of stories of adventure and some did the same as everyone else for their whole life. Who do you want to spend time with? Who do you want to be? To cross over to the 1%, you need to take chances, be brave, take risk, live with bravado.

Negotiate

You better learn this one. If you get a chance, observe three year old children and thirteen year old teenagers negotiate. If you can understand the essence of their negotiation ability you will be a master negotiator. I will give you some hints about what their magic is but it is best that you learn from observing them. (It is like if I tell you how to learn to ride a bike. You have to learn this experience, even with scrapes and bruises, on your own.) Never forget you learned to speak a language and walk by the time you were three so you can learn the skill of negotiating as well.

Three year old's and thirteen-year old's never give up when they want what they want. I do not agree with their ruthless, emotional tactics, which are sometimes brutal, but I respect their relentless drive to go after what they want, even if it is dangerous, risky and makes no sense accept to themselves. Learn from them. Learn what determination looks like. Find it in yourself.

They play the negotiation in two ways. Especially the three year old, they stay on point requesting what they want over and over. They keep the request simple and direct and they have focus.

"I want a cookie."

"It will spoil your appetite."

"I want a cookie."

"Maybe after diner."

"I want a cookie."

"If you behave."

"I want a cookie."

Three year old's escalate in volume and become more emotional. You are an adult so just stay with the part about "staying on point" repeat, keep it simple. Too bad. The loud part and the emotion part are very good at getting what you want but it is unacceptable behavior as an adult.
Thirteen year old's stay focused on what they want, but use more variety. They use guilt and manipulation ruthlessly. As an adult, guilt and manipulation can sometimes get what you want but it damages the relationship and chances for working together on another deal are ruined. Manipulation is good soap opera drama but bad for real life relationships.
Teenager's use a variety of tactics as part of their negotiation.

"I want to go to a party with my friends Saturday night."

"No, you cannot go there will be drinking there and you are underage."

"I know you drank underage, gramma told me."

"Yes, I made mistakes and I don't want you to go."

"You say you trust me and I have good friends. Are you saying that only to get me to like you better since you and dad separated?"

"I am not saying that to get you to like me. How could you say such a thing?"

"Then why not let me go to the party?"

Good adult negotiators have great people skills. Dealing with people, working together with others to create something greater than what you can accomplish alone, is a powerful tool. Good negotiators figure out who has the power. Who influences the decision, who controls the resources, who gets the job done? They see if they can get to an agreement. Best agreements are decided with regard to everybody getting a fair part of the responsibility and the reward.

You need to learn to handle the manipulators, con artists, bullies. This is a good lesson in life. Most people are honest but the nasty people in the world can cause exponential havoc in your life. It helps if you can spot them very quickly and do your best to never do a deal with them. If you are forced to negotiate with them, be strong, be the 'bull." With bully's weakness causes them to be more of the bully. Try not to get into the deal or work to get out of the deal. Use time limits, default clauses, back door escape routes. But if you can, walk away from the deal if you are dealing with a bully. (No run for your life.)

I have a friend who negotiates every day as part of his job. He is the gold standard of negotiation. I have never met anyone like him. He has the ability to know what you want more so than you know yourself and then he gives it to you. He accomplishes deals at the very highest level. He is one of the most loved people I have ever met and for good reason. He has a level of being intuitive that is like being clairvoyant. I am lucky to say that he is a friend. For him to be this understanding of others he must have to put so much of who he is aside and focus on the other in order to understand their desires, wants and longing. And then he gives people what they want in a humble way with no expectations. He is the example to aspire to. I believe when he negotiates, he gets to understand at a deep level what each side really wants and then he finds how to give to everyone their desires. His deals last. People give up the petty demands for the deeper hope of creating a meaningful union and a great business accomplishment.

Finding value

A friend bought the same size and type of house within two blocks as me and he bought his house about six months after I bought mine. He paid twice as much and he ripped out everything in the house and spent a fortune renovating it. His renovation was beautiful. He made very little profit and it was hard work and he has never renovated a space since. He bought high and sold not much higher than his costs. Interesting.

There is a catch phrase "buy low, sell high." Perhaps you have heard of it. I recently watched the stock market have an epic drop and after several months it went back to its value before the drop. Just before the drop who was selling and who was buying? After the market returned to its value who was selling and who was buying? Some people sold high; some people bought high. Some people sold low and some people bought low. Think about it. Which type of person are you?

Years ago, before I bought stock, I would talk to my friend Albert. From knowing his stock market buying record I knew he bought high and sold low. Albert is a very intelligent hard-working man and very good at his profession as a computer programmer. With the stock market he is pure crap. So, before I would buy stock I would talk to Albert. I would take him out for lunch and get a read on what he was doing about the market, buying or selling? I would do the opposite as Albert and Albert got a free lunch.

When looking for your "idea" of what business you want to consider there are a few concepts you should think about to help you decide what to take on. One idea is the buy low sell high plan. You want to look for growth potential. The money part of the growth is important but it is amazing to grow something, to make it more so. To influence something, put your intelligence, hard work, creativity forward and grow something. The financial increase is one symbol of your ability's success but there are more rewards to consider. Do you help others, or are you leaving something that is of benefit to others? Did you learn anything or did you improve yourself? Consider the start at the bottom and improve idea. It should be part of your process in your quest for the right project for you. Projects can be hard, bumpy sometimes not seeming to be rewarding in any way. It helps to keep in mind, not just the potential monitory gain but the personal growth and benefit to others to keep your motivation strong.

There are some ideas for looking at undervalued situations. A friend started to privately sell time for cell phone use. As his business developed, he kept hearing how people needed credit for purchasing the data for the phone. He realized that he could not only sell a data plan but he could piggy back on that business and lend money for purchasing data. This led to developing a loan business to help people who needed a short term loan to buy other items that they would pay back latter. He found the business connected to the business.

It is like the man who began to realize there was a business in making covers for cell phones. The business connected to the ever popular cell phone. Consider the aftermarket business around car sales, floor mats, car air fresheners, car seat covers and so on. This is a great idea, bet you wished you had thought of it first.

Look for something or develop something, that would be very useful. A service, a product that people did not know about, that people did not know was possible. Gadgets, toys, or services that can be crazy fun, imaginative to explore, to find an idea that could be developed. This calls for high end creativity, which seems the most interesting to me and the scariest for others. I always thought developing children's toys would be amazing. Just going to conventions where new toys are launched would be the best. Play time and imagination together with the great reward of tapping into the wonderment of children.

Consider situations that are a fraction of what they could be. I look for property that really could be double or four times what they appear to be. Having a legal address in a crowed city downtown is extremely valuable. To have a place that you can increase in size is undervalued. One building had twenty foot ceilings because it was a warehouse. What if this space was divided in half vertically and you could double the floor space? Add stairs and value. Air rights on top of buildings are very valuable whether you are building or just get permission to build, it is all increasing value. The excitement of dealing with city bureaucracy should never be under estimated.

Fast food companies figured this out. If they already had you at the cash register, they could, with a little nudge of persuasive talk, get you to give them more money. "Super Size Me." An increase in product size was a tiny expense to the company. The increase in price from the customer was low, but when you multiplied, this price bump by a million sales a day, was a tremendous profit.

Look for the situation where the product is not the value but the experience is the value. Farmers found their fruit crop was not as valuable as charging city people a huge fee to come and pick the fruit themselves. The charge for parking their suburban SUVS was more money than the money any farmer could image. The charging for entrance to the orchard to pick the fruit, the refreshment stand, the t shirt shop, the hay ride behind the tractor. Who knew the value was not the fruit but the experience in picking the fruit? The hardest part was for the farmers to believe someone would pay to pick the fruit. The farmers were used to paying workers to harvest their crop. It was outside of their imagination that anyone would pay for this experience. But the farmers came to the conclusion that city people were crazy and would pay for anything.

Put yourself in situations where new ideas are flowing past you. Read biographies about inventors. Get to know their thinking process that led them to the idea. Go to various trade shows where innovative ideas are on display. Go to unfamiliar places in your city, country, abroad and see thing you have never experienced before. Read the paper, especially the business section where developments in business and science are explained. Look for the new trending idea.

Exercise

Go find some ideas that you think are amazing.
A product or service connected to an existing service or product that could be developed.
Find an under valued product or service.
Find a service or product that is new that you think people would want.
Maybe the product is not the value but the experience is the value.
Look for something that could easily be doubled or made four times what it already is.

Work on developing your personal process to be open to new ideas. Where will you put yourself, what will you do, who will you associate with to be more open to new ideas, possibilities? This is an important part of developing your creativity.

The home run

You want the best idea you can possibly come up with. Not just any old idea for a business will do. Do the work at the front end of the project to create the very best idea possible. You need patience and stick-to-id-ness to find "this very precious idea." Do your home work, take your time, let the idea reveal itself to you and then hon your idea. Great is not good enough, spectacular is what you are aiming for. Once you have the idea, take the time to shape it. Smooth off the rough edges, find the idea's essence, in its purest form. The best idea is striking, simple, it resonates with people. Take the idea as far as you can and purify it. Then figure out how to make the brilliant idea work, the process, the mechanism to make it function. And then develop the mechanics of the process. Take out the noise, distractions, the roadblocks. Make it as seamless as possible. Root out the bureaucracy and then carefully put it out there for feedback and perk up your ears and listen.

When I first put my ideas out there, I received a great deal of negative criticism especially from people who were content to stay where they were in the 99% bubble. When I found a more enlightened crowd to spout my ideas their reaction was silence, which I took for indifference, perhaps boredom. This reaction was better than raw criticism. But I was wrong about people's reaction to my ideas. My best ideas caused people to think. They were taking the idea in, mulling it over. Then they would ask questions. Really good, thoughtful questions about the process to make the idea work. These questions were very helpful because they made me ponder the blind spots in my understanding on how to make the idea work.

When I did my first open house to rent a space I had created, I was surprised at the reaction. I liked what I created but people really got excited about what I had constructed. I took my time and developed the best idea for the space. I had no money so I created the space with the tiny budget I had. I pulled forward, highlighted the best features of the place and with my limited budget I added interesting forms. People at the open house asked if they could invite friends over just to see the space. People took pictures. People pulled me aside and asked if they could offer me more rent money than what I had advertised. They wanted to be at the front of the line. Two women who wanted the place together, said they were runway models, working in Paris and Milano thinking the glamour of their jobs would persuade me. I was worried that their sharp cheek bones would scratch the walls.

I got better at developing my ideas and putting them into action and with a budget I began to hear people gasp when they saw one of my renovated houses. I thought that only people with asthma were coming to my open houses. What I was doing was causing a visceral reaction. The spaces, moved people emotionally. People began to write essays explaining why they should be chosen to occupy the space. I would check for good spelling and grammar to help me decide who would get the space. Places began to sell for over the asking price, offers came in before places were for sale. It was paying off to be very thoughtful about what I created. I had no money so I had to rely on the best ideas and the best ideas for no money and the easiest to execute. But the feedback became interesting. People when they liked what I had done wanted to be part of it. They wanted to contribute their ideas, they wanted a say in the project, they wanted to be business partners. It was good to get feedback but it taught me to keep true to my vision and guard what I had created.

Synergy

"The interaction of the elements that when combined produce a total effect greater than the sum of the individual elements." The BAM! factor.

I was walking down a street one day with some friends in the oldest part of Havana Cuba and they knocked on the wrong door. We were greeted by a young man who said the house we were looking for was in the next city block. Five years later I am the business partner of this young man and we are changing the culture of the neighborhood where we first met.

What happened during this chance meeting? When my friend opened the door, I saw a beautiful court yard, an oasis of palm trees and lush gardens and beautiful freshly stuccoed walls. I asked to see inside this magnificent court yard, while the street outside had many buildings in need of renovation. My new friend was pleased to show off the extensive renovation he had completed from a ruin of a building. He gladly explained the details of the work he had completed and he had created an amazing bed and breakfast hotel. In Cuba, where it is very complicated to do construction because of an embargo, to find the construction supplies, tools and workman, this young man had made it happen. To start a business which was almost illegal is very complicated in his country but he got it done. I knew I had met an extraordinary man. Each time I returned to Cuba I would visit with my dear friend and he would tell me his next business project and I would discuss my plan to have a place in Cuba. I had been told many times that it was not possible to own a place in Cuba because foreigners are not allowed to own property in Cuba. I now have a three bedroom penthouse apartment by the ocean that I legally own and which gives me the right to do business and stay in Cuba as long as I wish.

What happened was that my Cuban friend asked me one day if I would help him with an investment with buying the third floor of a building. He had just bought into a building by purchasing the second floor. After much thought and listening to Frank Sinatra sing "I did it my way" eleven times. There was great risk involved and I needed Frank's advice. I said yes to the investment, but only if we also bought the first floor too. Synergy. The sum of the parts working together are more valuable than the separation of the parts. This ignited a drive with my friend and the project. The bigger idea where you capture the elements to create a powerful whole is a breathtaking idea. It is grand. It is a walk toward epic. Now the total renovation of the building could happen. Time had not been kind to the building but if you looked past the grim and the splintering stucco, you could see beautiful architectural detail that said this was a grand building built with care and love. The building is on a corner and its restoration would have an impact on how the surrounding streets. Changing the building back to its glory would make a statement of hope in a poor forgotten part of the city. Buying several other buildings along the radiating streets and restoring them would change the sensibility of the neighborhood. The new windows, restored stucco and wrought iron balconies created more than the restoration of this building, it was a sign of hope, a belief in the value of this glorious building and the neighborhood. Why just change the building, change the environment around it?

But then it was a chance to take the building and the neighborhood to the next level. We would make the building into a cultural center. We would have local artists show their work, have musicians play their music and dancers perform their routines. The building we restored would bring local artists together. This would bring tourists to our building which would also be a restaurant for wealthy tourists whose dollars would provide an income which would be used to hire local people and provide money for the arts. The two floors above the restaurant would have rooms to rent and again provide an income which would help fund the arts program in the building which would attract tourists. As the neighborhood changed the value our building and the buildings around it would improve.

I learned this lesson of synergy years ago when I met Josephine Jones. I was on my bike, riding through Harlem, on a cool November day. I saw a sign that said "Harlem Historical Society" in the window of a beautifully restored brown stone. I stopped to write down the telephone number on the sign. The door opened of the home and an elderly lady started to yell at me "What are doing?" We talked for three hours. We talked about her house and her neighborhood. Josephine told me that when she moved into her home during the 1970's the street was in shambles and dangerous. Her friends and family said. "Josephine, you are crazy lady." Josephine paid $17,000 for her house. Today her house is worth 6 million. "Josephine you are crazy rich lady." Josephine explained that she knew she could not just renovate her house she had to change her neighborhood. She said that the first thing she did to improve her neighborhood was she got rid of her husband because "that man was no good for nothing." Her street had a number of abandon houses which were used to sell drugs. The street had a lot of trash and forgotten broken down cars. Josephine organized the neighbors and they got the police to move out the drug dealers and got scrap metal dealers to hall away the cars. She got loans and grants from the city and state governments to help pay for the home's restorations. The architecture department at a local university she convinced to oversee the work. She had trees and flowers planted. Josephine changed her neighborhood. Now when the tourist bus goes by Josephine gives the bus the finger and yells, "Where were you when I needed you all those years ago?" But Josephine did not need the tourists she had her formidable self and her belief that she could make a difference. She knew that just changing her wreck of a house was not enough she had to go the extra distance and change her neighborhood, the environment that her house was in. Profound. Thank you, Josephine Jones.

I recently found a curious project. Commercial space usually sells for $1000 a square foot. But I found that a place in a great commercial area for $400 a square foot. What was the problem? Why so cheap? The space was in a mall that nobody went to. Few people came into the mall. Many of the commercial spaces sat empty and the few stores that stayed open had merchandise that nobody wanted. Shop owners looked bored and tired. Some were surfing the net others were reading the newspaper. The place was dead. But the mall was a good looking building in a very populated part of the city with many thriving businesses. It had only one way to go, this quiet commercial space because it was already at the bottom. What to do? What could the idea of synergy do for such a situation?

What if the mall became a destination space? What if it became a go- to- place to learn about new ideas for electric vehicles, bikes, scooters, motorcycles? What if new ideas about organic food, cooking techniques, wellness through nutrition were presented. What if green energy ideas were on display with knowledgeable people available to talk about break throughs in the technology. What if the mall became the place to go in the city where there was always something innovative going on? What if the stores were selling the products that complimented what was being presented? Bye bye dead mall. Hello cool, edgy, innovation place.

What if a team was developed with a wide range of expertise to rejuvenate the mall? A person who specialized on refurbishing commercial spaces and had a developed team of craftsman like a swat team, could quickly redo a commercial space making it engaging. What if a seasoned event organizer would plan the events, bring together the manufactures of the latest technologies and give them a space to show off their products and clever new technologies? What if a money guy was found who had experience raising money to build large residential and commercial buildings? He could develop a fund to loan money to current businesses in the mall to change the look of their space and buy new, more desirable inventory. Also, if a guy with extensive retail experience, buying direct from manufactures and selling through commercial space got interested in being part of the change in the mall, how good would that be?

Hiring this team was not an issue. Each of the team would buy into this space and make their money from selling a product in their space. The idea would be to buy into the mall at a low price and hopefully realize a capital increase in their investment as the culture of the mall turned into vibrate space. Also, their store, if successful would provide an income.

The idea is that you do not just buy into this mall at a low price for the unit, you change the sociology of the mall to change the environment around your space. You gather a team of various experts and you use their collective knowledge to recreate the mall. People love innovative change. It is hopeful, it is dynamic, it is very attractive. People want to be part of it. Synergy. Ride the wave.

You need to climb the ladder. You need to go up from where you are and see a different view point. Expand explanationally what you are creating and what you are. You need to open doors and go through to have different experiences outside of your familiar. Expand and be open to exceptional possibilities.

The franchise system is very much an example of this way of thinking. A business gets started, gets honed to a breath-taking idea with such great appeal that it is recreated in another location. It becomes a network of stores and perhaps, an international brand that transcends borders. A product that becomes part of a person's day to day life.

Music is like that. A series of sounds created so atoned to human psyche that it transcends languages and cultures. In Bruce Springsteen's autobiography he writes about being a good local band for the bars along the Jersey Shore. But he had a bigger idea. He wanted the "lightening in a bottle". He wanted to find that sound, that combination of notes that transcended the acceptance of his music, his talent, his craft beyond the Jersey Shore. He found it. Springsteen writes about being in a foreign country, standing on stage in front of thousands of people and they sing back to him the words and the melody that he wrote. What he had created was more than individual notes and words. He had created a sound that had in-bedded into the minds, hearts and souls of these strangers in a strange land. That to millions of people around the world for their whole life they would know the words and melody of what he had created and it would be an anthem for themselves and anthem that they would use to connect with others, forever.

How do you become open to this possibility, the chance meeting, the creation of a product, a piece of art that becomes so all encompassing you cannot forget about it. It is not possible. How do you find your inner Josephine Jones, Bruce Springsteen?

Instead of being negative, door closer, who keeps the blinders on, get your head out of a dark smelly place and open yourself up. Go outside of who and what you know. What you know has taken you this far, are you just working to stay inside a bubble that you have created or someone else has created for you. Take a step to the outside of the bubble, go exploring.

I have a friend Eric that likes to travel. When he goes to a new place, he does a deep, deep, deep dive. He opens the door very wide. When I first met Eric in Cuba, he had blisters on his feet.

“Why the blister’s Eric?”

“I walked from the airport to the beach.”

“Eric that is 14 km”

“NO no, it is 16 km according to the map.”

“Did you not have money for a cab Eric?”

“I had money but I wanted to know where I am and there is no better way than to walk and talk to the people.”

I met Eric because he was sleeping in a tree at the beach. He wanted to see the sun come up over the ocean in the morning. Eric went on to learn the Spanish language which helped when he married a local woman and this helped him become a citizen. Eric met a mutual friend who had written a tourist guide to Havana. Eric explained to our friend that he found her book helpful because, he could use the book’s pages to wipe his beautiful ass. Eric does not believe the tourist book is helpful. Get off the tourist trappings of where you are. Meet the local people, participate in their daily life, live the life of where you are. Eric is the 1% but without the money.

Eric does not stay at the tourist hotel and line up at the buffet or get on the tourist bus. He goes fishing for food with the local fisherman. He wanted to stay longer than the tourist visa would allow, so he married a local woman, became a citizen and moved in with her family.

Eric is an extreme example of going outside of the familiar and the predictable. But there is so much to learn from Eric. He puts aside what he is about. What he comes from, his culture, his language, what he thinks he knows about life and himself.

He embraces the unfamiliar circumstance that he finds himself and absorbs a new reality. Eric is open to people and the circumstances around him. He is not so defended psychologically that he pushes away people and chances in life. He gathers life experiences internationally. He is not stuck doing the same way of life with the same people for years. Eric does not know what being in a rut is about. Eric is also an accomplished medical doctor on the hard streets of St Petersburg Russia, when he is not marrying strangers in a strange land.

What can you learn from Eric, besides using tourist guides as alternate forms of toilet paper? It is possible to have a great life of adventure and possibility. Eric does not see the barriers to the life he wants. He knows that you can create the life and possibilities you want if you take the road blocks out of your way. You think your "No's" keep you safe. Your No's may just keep you in a rut and deny you possibilities or access to people and situations with knowledge to take you outside of your little 99% bubble.

Practice saying yes for a day or a week, month, forever. Stop talking about yourself and start asking questions, find your curiosity and start listening. Do not argue with people, take in their different ideas and think about them for a while. Put yourself in unfamiliar circumstance, read something in a magazine, book, newspaper that you would not usually read. Get to know, the other. Expand your travels, in your neighborhood, city, country, the world. Expand your possibilities. Be open to ideas. Watch for the connections that are possible between people, cultures, geographic locations. Keep in mind what you can bring to people. What is missing that you have access to. What do you know or have that is wanted? Get started on bringing this resource forward and connecting it to people. A food, an electronic device, a service. Start with it somewhere and see if it is so desired and appreciated that maybe it is wanted in many places by many people. Do not see limits, see possibilities. It is energizing to create. To hear back from strangers in a strange place something unique that you have created.

For twenty-five years on Saturday morning, I go to a place in the city where people gather for about twenty minutes. They pair off and run through the streets together. If you looked at the meeting spot before the 9am meet time and then twenty minutes later you would see nothing. Out of this group great friendships have formed. Couples have found each other and babies have been born. It is a well accomplished intellectual, educated group and great ideas have been shared about life, business and travel. But if you did not know when and where to look for twenty minutes once a week, you would not know this beautiful special group existed and you would miss a great opportunity to be part of it. What are you missing, what do you not see that is right before your eyes?

One of my favorite movies is the Bourne Identity. The hero of the movie has nothing. He wakes up out of a coma on a boat with strangers and he does not know who he is or where he comes from. He has no identification, money and he knows nothing about where he belongs. He becomes aware that he has some very specialized skills that help him survive in any situation. He is incredibly resourceful. In any situation he can find people, and things to help him find his way. In this culture I see an abundance of opportunity. It is everywhere. But many around me see closed doors, missed chances. A friend who is very intelligent and hardworking has nothing. Recently he told me his main source of transportation, his bike was gone. I said I would get him a bike. I kept my eyes open and a week later found a bike my neighbor had thrown in the garbage. It was missing a seat and the pedal crank did not turn. A little street market nearby sold random bike parts and a seat was found. With some oil the pedal crank easily began to move freely. A few adjustments to the brakes and some air in the tires and the bike was in good working order. I rode the bike around the city for a day and realized it was an extremely good bike with excellent mechanical parts. I gave the bike to my friend and wondered why he could not find what I found. What could I see all around me that he missed? Jason Bourne and I have so much in common. Who knew?

Ambition

An ambitious drone is a bad fit. You get a lot of negative attention.

Ambition is sometimes hard wired into a person's DNA. Ambition can be a curse or a blessing. A friend explained to me that he was always hungry for more. No matter what he achieved he was always looking for more. He explained that he was a grateful person for many of the things he had got out of life but he was always looking for the next thing to achieve. He wondered if his ambition could be cured with expensive psychotherapy or he could just go with it and enjoy the gifts he had earned along the way.

Ambition is defined as 'the desire for some object that confers distinction, honor, superiority, fame or power.' That will keep you busy. You are hungry for more. Power to influence seems to be part of the ambition. Being compliant, being content is not a mindset of ambition. If you are happy where you are this is a great place to be. But where you are, is that okay?

Can you create ambition? Maybe. What do you want out of life and do you already have it? If you do not have what you want what are you willing to do to get it. If the answer is nothing well that is the answer to the ambition question. If you look outside yourself for your ambition you are going in the wrong direction. No one runs a marathon for you. "I would run a marathon but my girlfriend won't let me and I need her to talk me into it." Thank you, I cannot stop laughing.

For some, the trail to your ambition is your anger. Are you under the control of someone or something and you are pissed off? Do you have enough anger to get you out from under repression of an unjust situation? If you have had to repress your anger out of fear, find your ambition to fuel your way out. Let your ambition stimulate your imagination to solve this problem.

Remember ambition is admired and despised. In many great stories the repressed victim heroine gets to the point that their survival relies on their rising up and taking back their life. They fight the good fight, overcome the most formidable obstacles and take back the control in their life. Ambition is the fuel for motivation.

Motivation

I did not want to write this chapter but I knew I had to. Why do it? What is the point of motivation any way, is it not just luck and what other people let you do, that is most important in getting things done? Nothing works out anyway so why bother? If you were to get into the 1%, people will be mad at you, hate you and make your life terrible. So why bother? The world is burning up, why create another planet destroying thing so you do not have to work and lay around the house all day?

Your motivation is probably your most important asset. If you have the most powerful car in the world mechanically, so sophisticated to reach the fastest speeds, but without a simple thing like gas, the best motor is nothing. You can be very intelligent with great skill, knowledge, luck and opportunity but if you don't feel like doing anything all that brain power is of no use. The terrible frustration of the parent of the teenager who tests gifted academically but only seems motivated to sit in the basement in their underwear, playing video games. It is very difficult to motivate others, even people you love.

Becoming part of the 1% means you need to change your way of thinking. How much of a negative pessimistic focus do you have? Do you avoid the anxiety of risk by making your decisions through the filter of a negativity? Is it most important to be right even if you get negative results every time? You make choices so things do not work out and then you can smugly say I knew it; it would not work. This is a pathological way to get self esteem. Being right regarding failure is a piece of crazy.

I think of watching a rocket take off for outer space. The most fuel is needed to break out of the gravitational pull of the earth. The fuel to propel the rocket outside of the earth's atmosphere is so much less. When you are in the rarified world of the 1% you are doing much more that you are motivated to do for yourself. Less constraints. It is a more motivating place to be. Breaking through the boundaries of being part of the 99% takes energy. Starting new behaviors, breaking old habits is hard. There is a big deferred gratification as part of this. Building a business is complicated frustrating and boring at times. The big payoff may be years away. Some are born with the sense of thinking and planning for the future and for some, now is all they can do. Breaking down activities into day-to-day accomplishments where you feel more immediate rewards, may be necessary.

It helps to know yourself regarding what sucks the life out of you. People don't realize that it takes a lot of motivation to stay inside the bubble of the 99%. You may find you don't really get anywhere new. Many jobs in the 99% category are rote, the tasks repeat with limited chance for personal growth and real accomplishment. You work to sustain not to create something new. Working on an assembly line creating the same product day after day takes tremendous self discipline and a practice of repressing any creativity. Working in many government jobs is a task to have a set of rules or restrictions enforced. Fill out this form, get people to adhere to the restrictions. Do you qualify or do you not, according to these regulations? How can you feel the joy, the inspiration, the creativity?

Doing things for people you do not like, who do not appreciate what you do sucks the life out of you. You empty yourself a little bit each time you do a task for the unliked unappreciated of the world. People by the time they retire, with their little pension are the walking dead with the life kicked the hell out of them. The worst is meeting someone a few years from getting their small pension and they have run out of gas to cross the finish line and get the barely life sustaining pension for their old age. They burned out so close to the finish line and they do not think they can make themselves go back to doing the job. It is a sad desperate situation. Hopefully with help they can find their motivation again and get where they need to go.

If there is no meaningful reward for your efforts you can deplete your sense of motivation. Motivation is like an investment account. Do you put your motivation into tasks that give back your motivation with interest, with interest compounded or with exponential growth? Or do you invest your motivation in something that depletes your motivational capital. Not only does it not maintain your level of motivation but it takes away your sense of motivation till you are bankrupt psychologically. You don't want to do the task or job you are required to do and you do not want to do much of anything. This is also called depression.

If you are often criticized for your efforts. This will hurt your motivation. If it is legitimate criticism then you need to up grade your skills and do the task properly. But if it is a management style to manipulate you psychologically to get you to work harder than this will demotivate you. If you are overly critical of yourself. No matter what you do, you find fault, or you have a perfectionistic streak, then you will hurt your motivation. If you are too dependent on your motivation from external sources, and you rely on overly critical people to get psychological rewards than you do not own your motivation. It is in the wrong person's hands.

If there is no psychological reward for your efforts this is not good for the psychological state of motivation. Money is not as good a reward as people hoped it would be. Same with material processions. It is a sense of feeling proud of your accomplishment, that has a greater meaning then the accomplishment of the task itself. If what you do helps yourself and more so helped others, it is the higher form of psychological motivation.

It is important in the task of becoming the 1% that you understand yourself regarding the issue of motivation. What motivates you and what takes away your motivation is important knowledge to have. To get to the 1% you are going to develop your motivation to overcome the gravitational pull of being part of the 99%. But this knowledge is more profound than it being the fuel to help you break free of the 99%. It is a piece of psychological wealth that is a profound investment in yourself. This knowledge is more valuable than the money you may get in your bank account. Motivation is more important than intelligence and ability. You can hire smart, you can hire talent but your motivation is the fuel that makes the big engine rev.

Exercise

Figure it out. What and who sucks the life out of you, leaves you tired and who and what revs you up.
Make a list, name names. Describe situations that energize you or wear you down.

To start developing your motivation consider how well you look after yourself physically? Do you eat properly and get enough sleep and exercise? Do you rely too much on additive chemicals, caffeine and sugar to give you a buzz of energy rather than the higher standard of a balanced diet. Is your environment where you live and work give you enough light, and comfort to keep you motivated? Do you spend three tense hours a day getting to and from work or is going to work a pleasant trip? One coworker instead of fighting rush hour traffic every day would often take his bicycle. It was faster and great exercise.

How do you reward yourself psychologically and with concrete symbols of achievements? It should be simple inexpensive tokens of rewards. Some over spend on their rewards. It is the simple act of congratulations not a $100,000 car that is the point of the reward. Day today rewards are the best. Time to listen to your favorite music, have a cup of tea, a walk in a beautiful park is the reward. Wear your favorite ratty sweater. Simple rewards, psychological symbols that represent a psychological reward stimulate your sense of motivation.

Seek out motivational people and situations such as people that truly compliment you for achievements, not for any manipulative gain. People that have a real appreciation for what you create. Do not try to provide a service or product for those who do not want it or do not need it. People who are on the same path as you and do not want to compete with you and there is a camaraderie, this is motivational. It is good to be part of a common cause especially if you are headed in the same direction and helping each other out. When you form a company of like minded people to develop a useful product this will charge you up. Reading books that motivate you is good. Biographies of people who are creative and overcome tough times are very motivational. There are experiences that are motivational. Situations that you have shied away from, but with some effort you have achieved. This can stoke your motivation with a sense of accomplishment.

The difference between Paul and Me.

I know a man, who is definitely part of the 1%. He has an incredible income and assets, knowledge and influence and all of that make him a leading candidate for the 1%. He does not need to work but chooses to and I do not know why. He is extremely successful at what he does but I never see any joy or passion for what he does. I wonder what his motivation is to work so hard at such a complicated level.

In considering what you take on as your project please consider the passion, the joy for the project. Some try to make a lot of money to prove something to others such as a dead relative that thought poorly of them. Perhaps they denied your existence and your value as a person. Maybe you are trying to prove something to class mates that ignored you in high school and thought you were a weenie and you want to rewrite their opinion of you. Some will be motivated to do well to prove something to people who never cared about you a long time ago and far away. You could do better than them and they may still will not care, because they are dead or that they do not care about much of anything but themselves. Its personal what drives you. Be careful if you are motivated in a way that is too connected to someone that has a history of hurting you or denies approval to you to manipulate you.

Fear of powerlessness and loneliness are negative motivators. Money and success will attract some people to you and you need to be careful about other's motivation.

Front end load the consideration for why you want to create a project that gives you economic freedom. Capitalism is what you are entering in a more extreme way. Our culture, law, society is a place of great opportunity that only a few takes full advantage of. Most people are middle class in their income and their choice of earning their income. And yet our legal, tax and banking system is designed to allow for great capitalistic opportunity. But few really go for it. For some, capitalistic philosophy is a slice of evil. The very few get rich on sweat and sacrifice of the many who will stay poor. There is some truth to this. Some wealthy people create slave labor work environments that take total advantage of many, deny them opportunities for education, and employment to keep people at the bottom and controllable. But you do not have to do it this way. Your project can have great benefits to others. You can offer economic opportunities for others, allow them to grow economically and for education. You could invest in projects that help others, be part of cleaning up the planet, hire homeless people or people who are difficult to employ. Capitalism is about growth. Creating something that did not exist before that can be a benefit to others. Your product could be helpful for people's comfort, efficiency, health, or entertainment.

Your project can be an expression of your highest values. It can have a philanthropy part and help through employment. The business can be an outlet for your creativity. Your day job turned out to be boring, have limited room for education and personal growth, but your project could be an ever expanding place of creativity and education. A place of action with limited bureaucracy.

Projects can be very hard and time consuming. It is helpful if they have a deeper meaning to you. If the project taps your esoteric morals and values. It will have a more profound meaning to you and you will be more motivated to see it through. Rather than be about work it can be about a quest. You will have to make many choices and decisions as part of building your project and if you have done thoughtful work at the beginning about why you are doing this, what you hope to accomplish, the many decisions will more easily be clear because you are following a vision for the project. You will know more instinctively the choices you need to make and what direction your project needs to take.

Belonging

Membership has its privileges unless you are never going to be accepted as a member. What if you are in a situation at work, or neighborhood, or relationship where you will never fit in, never be accepted. How much time and resources are you willing to squander to try to belong when there is great evidence that you are never going to be allowed in. Within the 99% there are a multitude of specialized groups. There are fractional groups in every culture. How much do you belong to the group? Sometimes the group has power and sometimes it is on the hunt for power. Sometimes it pathologically gets its power by taking it away from others in vicious self righteous ways. The more dependent the group is on the ones it is taking advantage of, the more restrictive, the more abusive they are. The slaves that kept the economy of the American South going were an example of tremendous dependency and tremendous abuse. Men that are abusive to their wives are often dependent on them financially, for household duties, and raising the children. They are very controlling, tell their wives they are no good, and that they cannot manage without them.

One abused woman explained that her able bodied husband used to sit on the edge of their bed every morning and swing his feet back and forth. This was the signal that before she went to work, she should get on her knees and put his shoes on his feet. He did not work but he made all the rules and commanded the household. One day she walked by him as he was swinging his feet and she kept going until she found a new place to live. He told her she would never survive without him. Her new husband is a kind man and earns a good income and he can put on his own shoes.

To belong should be a good experience with benefits that can only come with the resources of the group. But many belong to an environment that has a high price to be part of it. The herd asks too much from its members and provides none of the benefits of belonging. A healthy functioning group can provide a feeling of safety, mutual resources, togetherness and acceptance. The feeling of belonging is a powerful psychological draw for most people. We were not meant to be alone. But this need to belong is so powerful people will put up with a great deal of crazy and abuse in order to feel a connection. Part of abuse is telling a person they are no good, and restricting them from leaving, telling them that they are lesser than, but keeping them dependent on the group. If you are so worthless, why do they not set you free, be done with you? Is it because they are actually dependent on you? Inside abuse you can easily lose your prospective of what is real.

The dynamic of some groups is pathological. They create a group on their ability to exclude. The crazier the group the less it makes sense for who is in the group. The movie "Hidden Figures" is a great example. It appears that the group of mathematicians who were key in working through the math formulation for the NSA space launches were not made up of the best mathematicians. The criteria to be part of this elite group was not math ability, but gender and skin color, not math skill. How crazy was that?

Be careful not to believe that the elite group is the only way to have access to power and resources. It seems that way, but you may give up too much to try to belong to a group who do not want you and only give you a slim chance of ever being accepted and never allow access to any power or resources anyway. I, by chance went to hear the extraordinary actress Jane Fonda speak when she launched her biography. Ms. Fonda explained that by her early thirties she was not being hired by the movie studios anymore. She was considered too old and too controversial because her involvement in the Vietnam war. Jane started to develop her own movies and hired herself to act. She did not change to become accepted by the elite male movie studio group, she went out on her own to great success. Movies such as 'Coming Home' and 'On Golden Pond' were her creations. Very successful films.

If you are an ostracized minority within the 99% you can put a lot of effort toward fitting in. Scrapping off the edges of what makes you unique in order to be accepted, hoping you will be given some of the resources given to the others in the group. But this may not happen. If you are an outlier anyway, just go with it. The rules that are required to be accepted may restrict you from being all you can be. Fitting in is over rated. Finding your own path is way cooler and satisfying. If you are forced to be an outlier by the herd, then you are good to go. What do you have to lose when you are not given access anyway?

If you put all of your energy into finding your own resources on your own terms, resources that come directly to you rather than through some elitist group that wants to deny you access anyway, it is a cleaner more efficient way to operate. I recommend that you own your own economy, be the CEO, make the decisions, gather people around you who help your quest based on hard work and talent, not on stupid criteria that has nothing to do the requirements for the task at hand. Be careful that your efforts are to impress those who would not accept you. This is a waste of time and energy. Go out on your own for your own sake. However, when you make it on your own, those you left behind may beg you to come back and join the herd, with great promises of acceptance. Be careful. It's a trap. They can just take what you have, ditch you and tell you, you do not belong once they get what you have earned.

Exercise

Write out what makes you unique. How are you different from your coworkers, family, friends, and neighbors? What do you do to hide your differences? How much time and energy do you put into suppressing what makes you different and prove that you belong. Is It worth it? Seriously what do you get out of trying to fit in and do you get a good return for your effort. If it is not good for you, what else can you do with your time and energy.

Finding your voice

Say what? I am a pathologically shy person. Although I see the problems in staying quiet and distant from others, I chose staying quiet and in the background. It is unnatural to my personality to speak up, make a request from another. Unless I am burning up for something I want. But when I think about it, there are exceptions. I once stood in front of a large condo complex, in a foreign country where I did not speak the language and looked to meet someone from the building who might know of an apartment in the building that was available to buy. It was a lovely warm sunny day and my plan was that if saw anyone come out onto their balcony, I would call up to them and make my request. I was aware that the country I was in had reasonable psychiatric facilities and maybe that would be my plan b for housing, if an apartment was not available and the apartment's residence made a call for help if they deemed me crazy. Okay sometimes I 'am not so shy.

You need to find your voice. I believe that if you are going to make your way out of the 99% you need to speak up, ask for help, state your request, make your case, pitch your idea. You have things you need to say. People can speak the English language but they have a limited range of words, words that exist in the language but words they rarely use. "Can I have, I would like, please get this done." Asking for help, delegating, making requests, this is the part of the language that seems inaccessible for some. But it denies you access to opportunities outside of the 99%. Inside the 99% you take orders, you do not give them. You do not delegate, you listen to orders. You do things on behalf of others not for yourself. If you do ask for help or delegate etc you, do it on behalf of others, not for your own gain or your own purpose.

People are often raised in a way that they are told a million times that their voice is not to be heard and they are told that what they say is not going to be taken seriously. When you are older you can make requests, you can be heard as an adult but not now as a child. But if you do not practice a language when you are a child you will have a limited chance to learn it latter. This is true for having access to certain parts of the language you are learning. There are languages within languages. The part of the language that you delegate, ask for help, direct, and lead others may be an undeveloped part of your vocabulary. (Some will be horrified that I am suggesting that a four year old ADHD child get to direct the entire household like a CEO) Relax just let the little monster do that on Tuesdays. Ha Ha. How about pick a few issues that your child can practice at being the boss? An example would be their choice over what toys they want to play with and how. Yes, they will choose the pots and pans and make a big noise. You know where they are from the crashing sound they make. Steven Spielberg's mother would let him explode tins of soup on the stove so he could film the event and look how he turned out. But as an adult you need to practice using the part of your language where you command, ask for things, take charge, delegate. Pick an issue and practice making your requests. Have others and yourself hear your voice.

You may have your voice if you are asking on behalf of others but not on behalf of yourself. Your voice is a vital tool like your hands. Your words and the full use of the language are needed to help you get where you want to go. If you were lost and you did not have a map, but you had no words such as "where" in your vocabulary you could not ask for help. Developing a business, if it is something you have not done before means you do not know many things, you need to ask for help and it will be asking for something that will only benefit you. You will need to put in place a process that will make the business work. You will need to delegate. You will need to check for quality and you will need to criticize and ask for more. Is this part of the English language familiar to you? How often have you heard yourself use these types of words?

Back to my story about the condo where I wanted to buy a place in the country with the good psychiatric wards. It did not take long before I saw a man come out to his balcony on the third floor. By chance he was the president of the condo building and two of the building's residence had given him keys to their apartments because they wanted to sell their units. He spoke English well and after he showed me the apartments, we had drinks with several of his friends on his balcony. He and his friends were very helpful. They told me about the process for buying property in the building and about several other buildings in the neighborhood that had good units for sale. Sometimes when I find my voice it is a magical experience.

Exercise

Guess what you have to do?
You have to practice bossing people around. If you have to start with training wheels on, so be it. Choose someone or a situation that will cause you limited stress. Probably not your bossy mother-in-law or the neighbor who has a gun. What you want to do is hear yourself say the words. You want to practice commanding sentences.

"I want these dishes washed." "I want a $300,000 loan." "I need a list of who manufactures that item". "Where can I get that product wholesale?" "How did you get your business started?" "Set up that website so it gets the most traffic, by Tuesday."

Hear yourself say the words. Deal with the anxiety that comes up. Talk yourself through it. You might find that you like being the boss more than you thought. Watch out here you come and you are on fire!

Get stuff done.

I would never tell you to break the rules. That would be wrong. The law of gravity says you cannot fly. That is what is told to people getting on air planes.

You know what beats intelligence, good looks, favoritism? Getting stuff done. Having a goal and achieving it. That's the golden ticket. I did not have exceptional anything, or great acceptance by the A list. But I had the ability to get stuff done.

I love hearing Arnold Schwarzenegger talk on talk shows. He has great stories and a bravado rarely matched by others. Everything he wanted he got. He was told he could never be a leading actor in a movie. His name was too weird, he spoke with an accent and he had a strange physicality. His very successful leading man movie 'The Terminator' had an impossible low budget of six million dollars. Arnold described in an interview that they had no money for a studio set to film Terminator, they just filmed on the streets in LA "perhaps" without permits. He described how a scene called for him to punch out the window of a car and he just found a random car on the street and punched out the window. I am sure out of the six million, the film company paid for the window. The success of this movie was so great that the next budget for Terminator 2 was 100 million. Arnold is also a successful business man and owns a great deal of California real estate. He was also a successful politician. He gets stuff done.

I bought a piece of land with a building in an area where the city's rules said that a building had to be placed forty-five feet from the property's rear lot line. Also, the building must be five feet from either side of the lot. But the building lot I bought was forty-five feet long and ten feet wide and the existing building covered all of the land it sat on. The building had been built with a city building permit years ago. During one of the first meetings with the city, the city representative started the meeting by explaining the city rules for the positioning of buildings on city building lots. I was at the meeting to request that two more floors be added to the building. The land was in a historically protected area where no new construction is never, ever to be allowed. I write this from the finished addition that the city granted for the construction of the addition to the property.

Rules are important and they are created for very good reasons and it is important to our way of life and the survival of our civilization, that rules are adhered to.

I know some very intelligent people. I like the company of smart people, partly because I hope that their great intelligence will one day rub off on me and I will become a really smart person. I could not rely on super developed gray matter or whatever makes some one super crazy smart. I did not have that gift. I could ask some of the neuro scientists I know what makes some one smart. They think they know the answer to this question. But I often wondered what do I have that many do not. I get stuff done. It got to the point that I would dream up crazy things I wanted as a joke and I cannot stop laughing because some of things I said I wanted but not seriously, started to come to me. Be careful what you wish for is a lesson to be learned. For a while, as a joke I would tell people I wanted a building with a turret and an out building like a stable. Well damn it I got one. Even when I had no money as a down payment. If I want something, I go and get it and many do not do this. I am puzzled by what happens when people want something and they do not get it. What went wrong?

I remember my first experience of being in a car that had a GPS device. Very annoying. The chosen voice was set on whiny, bitchy, authoritarian. Very annoying. As we made our way to some obscure part of desert country north of Los

Angles this crazy device took us on more than a few roads that were a night mare. The driver, a very intelligent accomplished person was like a slave to this devise. He thought it knew best and we were to follow its commands. We were directed to a road where the bridge was out. I wondered if we were driving at night if we would have fallen into a dried up river bed. Or would we be stuck forever in a roundabout as the GPS voice commanded over and over "continue turning left" I guess if I ran out of vomit from being car sick that might have ended our following commands, but I am not sure. What is so hard about reading a map?

It seems a big quest to follow rules, no matter what. Do not think, do not see where you want to go, just follow the rules, without question or logic. Just the rules.

I have an older gay friend he explained that he was continually told that his physical and emotional connection to other men was wrong. There were laws against his thoughts and feelings. When he was growing up the laws said he could be fired from his job and be evicted from his apartment for being gay. He could never marry the person he was in love with. He came to the conclusion that he should work for himself, own his own home. He bought rental property and became a landlord. He had gay tenants and sometimes straight people, if they behaved themselves. Sometimes the rules don't make sense and sometimes the rules are abusive.

Perfectionism.

Perfectionism may seem to be in the way of getting where you want to go. The focus on the details, making them perfect seems to be the priority rather than the goal.

People with a lot of anxiety, worry and guilt seem to get stuck. They are more interested in their anxiety than getting where they want to go. They will put amazing road blocks in their way, impossible criteria before allowing themselves to go where they want, get what they desire. A friend explained that he wanted to have his family over to his home for a birthday celebration, but he could not have them over until he installed new hardwood floors. Not clean the floor, a little vacuuming, a dusting. No, the old floor had to be removed and an entire new floor had to be installed before any family gathering could possibly happen. Live inside that head.

With great guilt some people must suffer before they can have what they desire. There must be many hardships and sacrifices before anything can be had, or any goal can be achieved. If things come too easy there is great fear that it could too easily be taken away or it has no value. Complicated rituals only worthy of an obsessive compulsive disorder designation must be completed before anything can be achieved. If this is your lot in life you may find it easier not to have any goals. It's too hard.

Power

Gold and diamonds are just rocks. Many people decide they have value. That value changes. Not all people think gold and diamonds have value. Power is like that. Many people in a culture decide what is valuable, being influential has power. In the rural farm community where I grew up people believed they had power based on their choice of the livestock they owned. People that owned black angus beef cows believed they were superior people and had the right to have more influence, more power in the community. They believed and many others agreed that having this kind of livestock was a serious indicator of intelligence, hard work, morality, table manners, many many extraordinary virtues and thus you should be deferred to, given more power. Power such as where you could park your tractor when you came into town. If you were just a chicken farmer well you were not given as much power to choose over others and you got stinking chicken parking. What does he know, after all he is just a chicken farmer? He should park his tractor where ever a place is available. When I moved to the city nobody had livestock so it was a learning experience to know what were the symbols of power. What neighborhood you lived in, what car you drove seemed to be the cows and chickens of the city. Money in most civilized cultures has power because it influences. People do not walk around with amounts of money, they have symbols of it. What color is your credit card? Designer clothes, purses, cars, watches, shoes etc. There is an area of my city that every knows is the most expensive place in the city to have a house. Houses are built in this neighborhood in a way to impress. The view of the house from the street is meant to shock the visitor because of the scale of the home. The homes have intimating grandeur. This is more than just a place where you eat, sleep and go to the bathroom, it is designed to influence, it is a show of brutal power. Some laugh at these homes because they are ridicules and indicate the owner's childish attempt to impress others with extravagance. Others would be in awe of the owner because of what a home of this scale and ornamentation represents. They would allow themselves to believe the owner is wiser, smarter, more talented, some would defer to the owner of such a home. Cows verses chickens its everywhere. What impresses you? What influences you? Who or what has power, influence over you? What do you have power over?

A friend discussed with me his agony about which car he should buy. He wanted basic transportation but he was aware that the people he does business with will decide how creditable he is, because of his choice of car. A cheap car would mean that he is not intelligent, talented, or trustworthy. A premium expensive European car would influence people. It would give him more access to people and their ability to open doors for opportunities. He chose a three-year-old European brand name car. It was thirty-five percent cheaper because it was a few years old. He got the bling without paying full price and it would give him the same credibility. I told him to get a black angus cow to put in the back seat so people would really know he was important and he would get better parking.

Power is fickle. If you are part of the 99% you may believe you have limited power and in many ways you are correct. Because you are dependent on a wage given to you from a source you do not control, an employer. You are dependent. In the United States the employer also has control over your health care and this has a power that is part of why Health Care is not pushed to be Universal. Companies do not want to give up this extra level of power. You can see the boss, the company as having a great deal of power over you. If they are a benevolent boss and company, and treat you with fairness and respect. This power may be tolerable. But if you were to develop a source of income and a growing asset outside of your work place, it is not just the economic freedom you are going for, it is a "shift" in power you are creating. Think about it. If you did not feel worried or afraid in anyway about your dependence to your work place for your income how would that change your mind set about work. How free would you feel?

I was waiting with a man for a shipment of drywall for a construction project. This man's job was to unload the drywall from the truck and move it into the house. He had had this job for seven years. He was very relaxed easy going man. He askcd about the project and said he was looking to invest in a rental property because he wanted to make an investment. I assumed he had a fairly basic wage because he was an unskilled laborer in construction. I gave him the price point of rental property in the neighborhood thinking it would be out of his range. He said that the price point was no problem. Now I was curious.

"Where did you get your money?"

He smiled shyly and said. "Four months ago, I won a million in a lottery?"

"Why are you still moving drywall?"

"I am too young to retire, a million is not enough to not work and I like my job and the guys I work with. When I get my investments in place maybe I will change what I work at."

He was free to choose. He had the power to choose. There was something very relaxed, not afraid that comes when you have the power to choose. A shift in power had happened. He had power over his economics, he was free.

When the drywall arrived with his fellow coworkers, I understood why he stayed. They were nice guys, full of humor and ongoing advice for what their friend and coworker should do with his money. Very funny, very bad advice. (They told their friend he should quit work and keep his wife working. He had made his money, she needed to keep earning an income, that was her duty. I wonder what his wife's divorce lawyer would explain to her regarding splitting family assets?) Very funny guys.

Yes, you can develop an alternative source of income and asset building business or investment, but what you are doing that is more profound, you are changing the power you have in your life. You will begin to think of yourself in a different way and you will think of yourself differently as you relate to others. You will have more ownership of power, you will have the power to make more choices in your life. Important choices about how you spend your time and with who. You have the power to say no. A profound shift. Owning your own economy is one thing, owning your life is the bigger opportunity. Having control of your economic situation is a piece of having control of your life. What you have to do to build your own economy is the exercises, the training to build the psychological muscle to have the power to rule your life more effectively. You need to be more assertive, deal with people in a more effective way. Become more resilient to criticism, follow your own vision rather than the vision of the many. Finding your strength as an individual outside the protection of the 99%. Develop boundaries to protect what you create, your time, your resources, your beliefs. The 99% has a power because they are an over whelming mass, with collective resources that you are part of. To break from the herd, you need to be more self reliant, you have different access to the resources of the many when you find yourself away from them. You give up the power of the 99% when you go out on your own so you need your own source of power, yourself. Your talent, intelligence and work ethic are some of your powers. The bravest are those that stay in the herd and have their own sense of power. They do not wait to have the safety of their own economy before they act independent of the herd. Follow their own voice, agenda. They are the brave.

Exercise

When cake is being handed out do you get the biggest piece? Are you in the company of the person who always gets the biggest piece? Could you have the biggest piece but you always insist on giving the biggest piece away? Do you have the power to ask, demand for the biggest piece? Do you take turns getting the biggest piece or do you always defer?

What do you have power over in your life?
List what you have power over?
What do you want to have power over?
What do you have to do to get the power you want?
Who and what has power over you?
How okay are you with that power?
What is your personal power?

Luck

There is a person I know who has seen what I have done and explains to me that my results are due to luck, not hard work, creativity, or perseverance, just luck. He goes on to explain that anybody who had invested when I did would have the same results. Oh, the precious thoughts of the loud mouth fool. But there is a little bit of truth in the village idiot's words. Luck is a factor in success.

There is the story of a simple man who prays every day that he will win a lottery. He prays and prays. And one day when he prays, he says "I have been a good man, I follow the commandments, why not grant me this one favor, please let me win a lottery." The heavens open up and a loud booming voice calls out. "Could you please, at least, buy a lottery ticket."

Yes, luck is a factor and what is luck? Some think luck is out of your control and some believe it is something you can influence. I believe you cannot control everything and I have given my all to try to control as much as possible. What you can hope for is to influence. A friend started a service business. He provided a great service and anyone using what he had to offer got great results. But like many small businesses, what was lacking was marketing. Many people offer a product or service that is excellent and is a reflection of hard work and quality and is based on an expertise or talent but what is lacking is the marketing. People don't get it out there. It is surprising how many people have a shyness. It is built into the culture of the 99% the idea to shun attention and this is a huge draw back to the success of a business. No attention here please, nothing to see, blend in, no limelight for me thanks very much. Well, you have work to do. Marketing is an influencer to the luck of success and successful luck.

Marketing is asking for attention and it is saying you have something that is special, better, something exceptional. It is not saying you have something that is ordinary that just fits in, that it is part of the rest. It is against the grain of the thinking of the 99% that they have something special, extraordinary because if they did, they would not fit into the 99%. As part of coming out of the culture of the 99% you have to break out of the "don't look at me", kind of thinking.

Also, to influence your luck you are going to need the help of others and their beautiful special knowledge. You only know what you know and what you know is not enough to get you out of the 99%. You have to connect with others who have information and ideas to launch you outside of the 99%. You will have to ask for help. The 99% offer help with what knowledge they have, but to get outside of where you are you will need to ask the 1% what they know. Often the 99% are taught that they cannot approach these special people. They are like secrete cows. They are too important, too busy, too special for you to go near them and certainly do not ask of them. But the 1% know stuff you need to know in order to join them. If you are going to improve your luck, knowledge is an important factor. If you were going to go to Vegas to gamble with your money with your limited knowledge of gambling, good luck. Or you could talk with the 99%, the people who are as likely as you to lose their money as fast as you and find out about their lucky rabbit foot theory, turn three times to the left and cough on the dice theory, or you could seek out the person that knows game theory, counting cards and playing the odds. Oh the 1% of better than average winners. These are the people that influence their luck with knowledge. So, you have to go to seek out and ask for the knowledge. You also have to expose the fact that you are trying to better yourself, that you are looking to become more, that you want to be successful.

There it is, the word SUCCESS. Are you okay? Sit down, breath, the word is part of the language. Is it part of your language? It is a foreign word for the 99%. It is outside of the part of the language they are used to. Fit in, make due, mediocrity, average, those are the acceptable words of the 99% culture. I always wonder how it makes sense to buy certain cars that have absolutely no sense of style, no design, no esthetic. Plain, drab, as unremarkable as possible. If by chance I make a wrong turn and end up in a suburban housing development and I am on a street where the houses are all the same, I wonder, were architects banned from the project? Street after street of the most unimaginative pile of bricks possible. I wonder, how is this possible? Who bought this crap? Clothing choices that say, I do not care about myself, my life, about anything. Why are they chosen? There is a sensibility in the 99% mentality to blend in but success in business requires that you stand out.

I think some people make choices to fit in, to indicate they are part of something. They do not want to draw attention to themselves. They make choices so they do not stand out. They are camouflaging, blending into the forest. It seems safer to go without attention. But to say you want to succeed puts you in the place outside the herd. You are the soldier with a bright red uniform like a bull's eye. I always look for the red door. If I get lost in a suburb sprawl and all the houses are similar and ordinary, I look for the one brave suburbanite who painted their front door red. It stands out. It is different. It's a try.

It's okay to ask for more than the average. To give yourself permission to want more, to try for extra, for different, for better than the rest. You have to face your fear of attention, self-esteem issues and judgement of people who are different.

Also, to improve your luck you need to market yourself. Put yourself, your product, your service out there to be noticed. You must also show you are better than the rest, superior, more successful. Words that go against the grain of the culture of the 99%. But you need to influence people's choices to improve your luck. Getting attention, self-promotion is part of influencing choice. Too many in business hope for the best. They launch their product, their service and they pray for a divine intervention of attention. But to give yourself the best chance, the best luck you need is to promote. This may be an unnatural ability, an undeveloped skill. Well time to learn. Many talented artists face this problem. Great artist, no promotional skill. How much great art stays in the studio, not given the light of day or the attention required to be given public awareness.

My daughter when she was eight would stop at kids' lemonade stands and try the lemonade that was being served up. For a while I thought she was just thirsty on these hot summer days. But I began to realize she was taste testing. She approached me one day and requested that she wanted to make a lemonade stand. She did not just want to make some money, she just wanted to put a product out there that was better than what she had been tasting from the neighborhood kids. (I get first crack at her IPO). The night before she set up the lemonade stand, she made up samples of lemonade till she got the flavor she thought was best and then she made brownies and requested I get gummy bears. I asked. "Is the lemonade not enough?" She explained to me that if she already had the kids wanting to buy the lemonade, they would probably be open to buying the "other stuff as well."

The next day as I was getting ready to haul the table for the lemonade stand outside my daughter stopped me and requested, I photo copy a sign she had made. "Great Lemonade for Sale, Gummy Bears and Browns too." She explained to me that we needed to advertise. After I ran off the copies, she instructed me where to post the signs. I am her first employee. I hauled the lemonade table and product to the side walk and started to set up when my daughter had more ideas.

"This is the wrong place daddy."

"Where is the right place my dear?"

"Across the street near the playground where the children are playing. They will be all sweaty from playing and will need a cold drink."

A dull normal child is so much easier to raise. Just put them in front of a television and they are fine. I have to step up every day with a child like this, a child who has an appetite for life. I am grateful and I need a rest.

My eight year old darling child knew to not just have a great product but she needed to advertise and she needed to place herself and her product front and center for her audience, for success. She did not rely on luck to sell her product. She developed a great tasting lemonade, better than the stuff the other kids in the neighborhood were offering. She influenced the chance of it being sold by advertising and she positioned herself in the best location for people to find what she was selling. Try to keep up people to the eight year old.

Resilience

When luck runs out, when best laid plans fail, when the going gets tough, when there are two sharks, not just one what are you going to do? Life happens. Who are you going to be? Go down fighting, cut your losses and run. Take a wrong turn, don't look back. Are you going to have stories to tell? Will you have hard won wisdom. The best stories have drama and heroes. The best stories have impending disaster and the fight out of the depths of despair. If you hide under your bed, you may just choke on the dust. When you die don't you want them to need time to pick up the pieces of you?

When you take risk there is going to be trouble. You are going to get blindsided in an unpredictable way. When you thought nothing else could go wrong, the lights went out. You get to find out what you are made of, what you are capable of.

I found out that my house, the one I had put everything I had into, had the most contaminated soil in the neighborhood. I found out at an open meeting, attended by hundreds of people from the neighborhood, including my tenants. All eyes turned to me when they made the announcement. Nowhere to run to. Nowhere to hide. You find out if you have friends. Smell the blood, see the sharks.

You can read how to be resilient but the best is to find yourself in trouble and figure it out, talk yourself through it, find your strength your abilities and survive. You get tested. Your best chance is to stay optimistic. Push away and contain your negative disaster thoughts. Stomp your foot and say "not now," because you got stuff to do. Focus on finding a way out, survive. The coal mine you work in just collapsed around you. Do you think "That's it I am going to die". Or I will stay busy till they rescue you, I will train for the New York marathon while I wait for the rescue team to get me out of here."(true story of a trapped miner in Chile)

Yes, sometimes there is a needle in a haystack. So, start digging. Ask for help. You need it. Find your voice. Get a professional who is an expert at needles in hay stacks. I am sure they exist. And even with an expert, dig in and find resources to help them. Get the biggest metal detector there is. It's your problem, the two sharks, the bad soil, the missing golden needle. Get in there and drive from behind to find the solution.

I missed the plane. People were waiting for me, no way to contact them. I never miss a plane, that is what my irresponsible cousin Ned does, not me. I ran so fast. I found the last flight out. Not easy, Not impossible.

A letter to my daughter

With my lovely and adorable daughter, I visited a castle that a man had built 100 years ago. It is a grand manor, with turrets and secret passage ways, enormous rooms fitting a king of a minor fiefdom. But the story goes that he lovingly built the castle, sparing no expense for himself and his wife and he only lived in the place for a few years. My daughter and I watched a video presentation at the castle which told the story about the great man and the video explained that he lost his great fortune.

My daughter turned to me and asked. “Dad why did the man not live in his castle for very long?”

I tried to explain, but I did it badly, “he made some bad business decisions.”

My daughter looked me in the eye and said “Daddy did he spend all his capital, because daddy, you know, you should never spend your capital.”

She was ten years old. That’s my dear adorable child.

What I want to tell my daughter, what I want her to know, is how to have as much freedom as possible in her life. I want her to know how to put herself in a place where she has the most and the best choices life has to offer. She is growing up in a culture that offers many opportunities to make this possible. As a woman she may have the responsibilities of providing for children and be in a vulnerable position to have to care for her children and to provide for herself at the same time. I wish for her to have advantages, not compromises in her life. Where she gets to make the best choices for herself and never out of financial scarcity be between a rock and a hard place. Not only do I want for her to be secure financially, but to have the knowledge to always provide for herself no matter what happens in this culture, economically and politically. Her having a big trust fund is not enough, she needs to have the knowledge to build her own economic empire. I want that she is never stuck in a demoralizing relationship or job for financial reasons. She can have the knowledge and therefore the power to be free of any power and control from others.

My daughter is very intelligent, and creative. She is very lucky and so am I. She is blessed. I made a decision when she was very young to expose her to many worldly opportunities, many of which took some economic clout to experience. When I realized how intelligent and creative, she was I thought I could give her a big life because I knew she had the ability to create this for herself. I was aware of some people who were raised in wealthy families but were not intelligent or hard working enough to create the life they were born into. They would always be dependent on their family to maintain them financially so they could afford the lifestyle they were familiar with. For these kids, they only knew their friends and family through exclusive private schools, country clubs, ski resorts, and other expensive social activities. They could not afford their life on their own. The embarrassment of not being able to afford a rich life style would be too much for some and they would not have been socialized for a simpler economic way of life. The joy of a baloney sandwich would not have been found if you were used to caviar.

I wish for my daughter to get a great education and prepare herself for a regular job and a career. I hope she finds a job inside a good company where she learns to be part of an organization that accomplishes great things with the efforts of a hardworking, talented group of people. The middle class values and work ethic are important to develop in a person. Show up to work on time, work well with others, create something that only a group of people can accomplish. To have great self discipline to work on something with others when you do not always understand the purpose. To know what it feels like to be a cog in the wheel. To know how to follow, do boring stuff, work inside a bureaucracy, do what is expected of you. I wish this work experience for her because it is part of knowing this reality for most people. It is their destiny for their working career and to understand it and learn from it and decide if it is for you or she needs more.

My first job as a laborer was grueling. The notice on the bulletin board that greeted me my first day of work said "only through long hard back breaking work is there salvation." I found salvation by noon my first day. I saw the job through and in the long run I am grateful for not quitting and choosing the easy way out. I would not wish this tortuous experience for my daughter or on anyone else, but I wish for my daughter to find her best self. She should develop her best self and her own economy outside of a collective work experience.

My daughter has the great advantage of time. It is not how much you invest but the more important factor is how much time you have to invest it. (Do the math. $1000 invested at 5% at age 20 until you are 60, when the money earned is reinvested, because you should never spend your capital or $1000 invested for ten years from age 50 to age 60 =). So, what do I want her to know?

My daughter now is a teenager and she knows everything and I embarrass her and I smell. Good, this exactly what she should be thinking. She is right on schedule to grow up and find out who she is as she develops her own lovely self outside of who I am. In her early 20's when she is on her own, she will be in the 1-1 economic level and I hope to give her some seed money to jump start her out of this level of functioning. But she must do the work to find her idea, through something she is passionate about. A business, a product, a service, some investment that she can begin to grow into an independent source of income for herself. The first step is to know herself well enough to know what she is passionate about. Something she is driven to develop. She needs to tap into her creativity to find what she is not just interested in, but passionate about to explore and develop. I wish for her to meet the challenges along the way of growing such an investment. To grow the resilience needed to overcome the criticism of people trying to hold her back, doubting her idea, trying slow her independence, her own power. I wish she learns to handle risk. To learn risk management to safeguard herself and the idea she is developing. Test out her ideas and see them through, learn to get things done and know her process to accomplish things. How she can stay motivated, and keep her belief in herself and her ideas even when things are not working. I hope she finds her voice to ask for what she wants with the full range of the English language. The language of leadership to ask for, command, and encourage those around her for a common goal that can only be achieved with the collective of a group. I hope she creates something she can be proud of and something that helps her grow as a person, develops her abilities and gives her great personal power. Something that helps other people in a meaningful way.

Last chapter

I hope you learn about yourself. I hope you became more self reliant, and find more resources in yourself. I hope you find that you can develop an idea and resist the pull of the 99%

and to act on your idea. I hope you find a process to develop your creativity and develop an idea that could lead to your economic freedom. I wish for you to expand your economic possibilities. Learn to be more resilient to the pull of the 99%. More immune to criticism, develop your stick-to-id ness in light of approval and acceptance. Develop your ability to lead and be more guarded about what is important to you, your ideas, time and talent.

Your first idea for developing your own economy may not give you the money for your economic freedom, that is the icing on the cake. The cake is your personal development along the way. How you grow as a person, this is the greater value. Patience is a virtue when developing a business idea. Personal growth, knowing yourself better is the true gain. Knowing how to motivate yourself, how to spark your creativity are very important lessons to learn.

I remember being at city hall in a planning board meeting, it was my birthday and I had ten minutes to present my request for dividing my property into two separate addresses. The location of the property was such that a legal address was more important than whatever structure was on the property. Dividing the property in two doubled the value of the property. I had been told that it was not possible to divide this property in two. It could not be done. It was impossible. I presented my case. The people on the planning board looked at the drawings of the property. They looked at me. They whispered to each other. They cast their ballots, yes or no and the Committee Chairman counted the ballots and looked me in the eye and said. "Yes". Happy birthday for the rest of my life. I added so much value to that property, which had a great income, that I knew I never had to work again in my life. This property would work for me. Thank you. I was free. It is like having the winning lottery ticket accept you developed a winning lottery ticket machine and you had the knowledge to do it again and again. It is a life time achievement award. Congratulations.

But if you get the icing and I hope you do, it is amazing. There is an expression called "going over the wall." For those that broke free from the 99% and crossed that magic line to becoming the 1% they remember that magic moment. They remember when and where they were. They knew they were free. They were no longer obligated to any one or any work place economically. They had the freedom to make the most beautiful choices that made sense to them. They were free of the influence of a work place or any individual they were in a relationship with where a financial obligation was part of the connection. Financial freedom changes the dynamic with people you work with and friends and family. It also changes your relationship with yourself. How you think of yourself changes. You may feel your body relax in a way that you did not know it could. You may feel muscles unwind that you did not know were restricted. Hopefully all that you learned along the way to get you financial freedom helps you stay where you are and helps you resist the pull back into the 99% from yourself and others. Some go back to the 99% be careful. Boundaries.

There are joys of being the 1% that are not well known. The joy of helping others is profound. There is a stigma that the 1% are greedy money hungry criminals that have squeezed the poor out of their money. Calm down. This may be true for a percentage of the 1% but the stigma is bigger than the reality. The joy of giving to others, to help people is beyond any joy of buying stuff. Helping people get where you are, helping them be more self reliant and not just helping them for the moment is very good. When you have faced the process of learning to be self sufficient economically it is probably within you to help others achieve this as well. The concept of the micro loan to start small businesses is a great idea to pursue.

But the greatest accomplishment is to develop your beautiful self to take yourself out for a test drive and see how far and how fast you can go. To find out what you are made of, what you are capable of. To become more than you dreamed possible. (It is fun to become more than others dreamed possible for you.) To live with the most freedom and enjoy the best this life can offer you. I wish you well.

Bibliography

Amornso, Sophia. “Girlboss,” Penguin New York, 2014.

Bach, Richard. “Jonathan Livingston Seagull.” Macmillan. New York. 1970.

Bacharach, Burt. “I’ll Never Fall In Love Again.” Scepter Label. 1969.

Fonda, Jane. “My life so Far.” Random House, New York. 1985.

Hemingway, Ernest. "The Old Man and The Sea," Charles Scribner Sons, New York. 1952.

"Hidden Figures" Director Theodore Melfi, Dec. 10, 2016.

Ruz, Guy. "How I built this," NPR 2016.

Schwarzenegger, Arnold. "The David Letterman Show," New York, 1985.

Springsteen, Bruce. "Born To Run," Simon Schuster, New York, 2016.

"The Bourne Identity," Director Doug Liman, Production Co. Kennedy/Marshall, 2002.

"Thomas The Train," Created by Christopher Audry, 1984.

www.ingramcontent.com/pod-product-compliance
Ingram Content Group UK Ltd.
Pitfield, Milton Keynes, MK11 3LW, UK
UKHW022021190726
13853UKWH00005B/2039

9 798515 855321